PORTRAITS OF THE
RAINFOREST

PORTRAITS OF THE
RAINFOREST

ADRIAN FORSYTH

PHOTOGRAPHS BY MICHAEL AND PATRICIA FOGDEN

ROBERT HALE · LONDON

First published in Great Britain 1991

ISBN 0-7090-4487-9

Robert Hale Limited
Clerkenwell House
Clerkenwell Green
London EC IR OHT

Published simultaneously in Canada by Camden House Publishing (a division of Telemedia Publishing Inc.)

Printed in Canada

Front cover insets from left to right: Red-eyed leaf frog (*Agalychnis callioryas*); golden beetle (*Plusiotis resplendens*); parrot snake (*Leptophis depressirostris*).

Back cover insets from left to right: Passion-vine butterfly (*Heliconius cylsonimus*); pupa of ithomiine butterfly (*Thyridia psidii*); plain tree snake (*Imantodes inornata*).

Design by
Linda J. Menyes

Colour separations by
Hadwen Graphics
Ottawa, Ontario

Printed on acid-free paper

This book is dedicated to the memory of Barbara D'Achille, journalist, environmentalist and friend. In her effort to communicate the natural beauty of Peru to its people, D'Achille made the ultimate sacrifice for conservation.

The author would like to thank the following people, agencies and organizations for providing assistance and information: David Bell, Jim Crisp, Chris Darling, Cynthia Echevarria, Michael and Patricia Fogden, Turid Forsyth, Wolf Guindon, William Haber, Bruce Lyon, John Terborgh, Conservation International, the Monteverde Conservation League, the Peruvian National Park System, the Tropical Science Centre, World Wildlife Fund Canada and Camden House's many employees: editor Tracy C. Read, art director Linda J. Menyes, copy editors Catherine DeLury and Lois Casselman, typesetter Patricia Denard-Hinch, editorial assistant Jane Good, publishing coordinator Mirielle Keeling, production manager Susan Dickinson and associates Christine Kulyk, Mary Patton, Charlotte DuChene, Laura Elston, Ellen Brooks Mortfield, Jennifer Purvis and Christina Tracy.

Michael and Patricia Fogden wish to acknowledge their indebtedness to Peter Jenson of Explorama Tours, Iquitos, Peru, for generously providing accommodation at Explornapo Camp and Explorama Lodge in the Amazon region of South America and for facilitating their photography in other ways.

CONTENTS

8
FOREST OF DREAMS
A Foreword by E.O. Wilson

10
PREFACE
Flower for a Day

14
ROOTS OF DIVERSITY
The Origins of Tropical Variety

24
FROGS
Life History Strategies
in Rainforest Amphibians

34
RARITY
Why Rare Species Are
Common in the Tropics

42
THE ESSENCE OF SNAKE
The Foraging Tactics of Serpents

52
FRUITS OF REASON
Interpreting the Meaning
of Tropical Fruit

60
TAILS OF GLORY
The Ecology of Prehensile Tails

68
SALTS OF THE EARTH
Nutrient Cycles
in Tropical Forests

74
HERMITS & HELICONIAS
The Microcosm of Plant
& Animal Coevolution

84
THE USE OF MAGIC
The Making of
Indigenous Knowledge

98
THE HIDDEN
The Adaptive Coloration
of Prey & Predators

118
THE VIRTUES OF SLOTH
Adaptation to
Life in the Canopy

136
EL TIGRE
Why Jaguars Are the
Ultimate Predator

150
FURTHER READING

152
INDEX

92
TERMITES & TAMANDUAS
The Role of Wood Eating
in Tropical Ecology

110
FISHES FAT & FIERCE
Encounters With
Underwater Amazonia

126
BEETLEJUICE
Chemical Defence by Insects
& Other Arthropods

142
BEYOND THE GUN
A Journey Into Virgin Amazonia

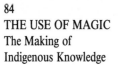

FOREST OF DREAMS

A FOREWORD BY E. O. WILSON

Conservationist Aldo Leopold's observation that the ecologist lives in a world of wounds bears a special poignancy with regard to the Tropics. Already, virgin wilderness is almost unattainable. To watch a naked Amerindian stand in an unpolluted stream and hunt fish with bow and arrow in the Pleistocene manner, as Adrian Forsyth has done, requires both determination and luck.

The Stone Age peoples of the world who have managed to survive influenza and venereal disease are down to a few tens of thousands and are being quickly furnished with guns and Disneyland t-shirts even as they are driven from their land. The forests around them are felled and burned with greedy abandon. The tropical rainforest today covers only 6 percent of the land surface of the world, down nearly half from its original extent. It is being removed at the rate of about 1 percent a year, or 100,000 square kilometres (equal to the size of a football field per second). Put another way, the rainforest covers an area roughly that of the United States, and human activity is destroying an area equal to that of South Carolina each year. *Portraits of the Rainforest* is thus in imminent danger of becoming more a historical document than a Baedeker of the tropical environment.

Why should anyone care? That is the point of this collection of essays. An academic ecologist with long experience in the Tropics, Forsyth contributes with this book to the genuine literature of ecology, wherein exact knowledge is expressed through the prisms of disciplined emotion. Such writing requires a rare combination of scientific training and metaphorical skill, and Forsyth displays the instincts of a creative writer, taking us deep into the tropical rainforest.

Most of the world's biological diversity, as Forsyth points out, lives in rainforests. Biologists have described and put scientific names on 1.4 million species in all parts of the world, but they emphasize that this is only a small fraction of the actual number, which probably lies somewhere between 10 million and 80 million. With more than half of the species residing in rainforests, it can be conservatively estimated that more than one-quarter of all the species in the world will vanish during the next 50 years. To see what that means close up, consider the amazing density of life and the restricted distribution of plant and animal forms described by Forsyth in the mountain cloud forests of the eastern Andean slopes. When a mountain ridge in Ecuador was recently cleared — a routine operation nowadays in South America — 38 plant species limited to the ridge at once became extinct.

Palaeontologists have recorded five episodes of mass extinction during the past 600 million years, the length of time spanning the history of modern life forms in the sea and on land. The present spasm, which includes the destruction of rainforests and other rich natural habitats, is the sixth episode and potentially the most dangerous for life as a whole: not only does the cut promise to be deeper, but for the first time, even plant species are being eliminated in large numbers. A further warning: The average life span of a species and its descendants in the past has been from 1 to 10 million years, depending on group. The time required for the loss in diversity to be restored by natural species formation following previous episodes has been 5 to 10 million years.

All this tells us that humanity is carelessly throwing away the Creation and relinquishing the chance to regain it. In order to appreciate the magnitude of that loss and to stanch it so that future generations may not curse our name, we must learn more about life on Earth, and we must learn it quickly. The tropical rainforest is vastly more than jungles and bugs. It is a treasure house of resources and a cathedral of organic complexity. It will be a potential source of wonder and an aesthetic thrill for all time to come if we refrain from burning it down and letting it wash to the sea.

For these reasons, *Portraits of the Rainforest* represents much more than simple nature writing. It calls attention to the best of this planet and to the compelling reasons why we should look south, inland, to the forest of dreams. Then we can remember in the deepest sense where this race came from and why life itself, and not just Earth, is home.

E.O.W., Harvard University, April 1990

Hyla ebraccata, left, is one of the hundreds of species of rainforest frog adapted for climbing through the vegetation; it even lays its eggs on leaves. Like many tropical insects, the adults of these flag-footed bug nymphs (*Diactor* spp), centre, possess toxic defensive secretions. The passion-vine butterfly (*Heliconius hecale*), right, makes early-morning visitations to the *Lantana* for pollen.

PREFACE

FLOWER FOR A DAY

A spring morning here is announced by the loud, excessively cheerful chorusing of the clay-coloured robins that forage in the patch of pasture below the cabin. Today, their rudely saccharine effect is tempered by the hoarse, rumbling protestations of howler monkeys in the forest that surrounds us. I feel the way the howlers sound this cool morning. My damp field clothes are clammy as I pull them on over stiff limbs. The sun still hides behind the eastern hills, and hot coffee is sorely needed. Photographer Michael Fogden, the owner of the accommodation, attends to this dependency first. Soon, we are outside on the birding bench that overlooks the mountainous landscape, hands cupped around warm mugs, letting the infusion of sugar, caffeine and complex alkaloids do its vitalizing work. There is no need to move just yet. From this perch, Michael has identified some 220 species of bird, and two hours of excellent, completely sedentary birding lie ahead.

From the porch, I can see that it is a rare day, a *Sobralia* day. Below us, the landscape is one vast composition imbued with every shade of green. But this morning, the tree crowns are emblazoned here and there with clumps of huge, white orchid blossoms that catch the morning sun. They are *Sobralia*, massive orchids that bloom en masse for one brief and unpredictable day. By tomorrow morning, the fragile petals will have faded; they seem to self-digest once their single day is done.

Overhead, a flock of parrots races, calling out the sound of the Tropics. Without looking, Michael identifies them as brown-headed parrots — birds distinguished by voices more musical and less raucous than those of other parrots — and I try to absorb both the sound and yet another bit of Michael's ornithological expertise. We watch a succession of small birds taking rewards that plants normally confer upon ants. A scarlet-thighed blue dacnis drinks at the extrafloral nectaries of an *Inga* treelet sprouting up in front of the porch. The *Cecropia* tree, which produces tiny white Müllerian bodies in brown velvet glandular patches under its leaf stems for the *Azteca* ants that defend its leaves, is being robbed by seed eaters, bananaquits and parulas that pluck the bodies with rapid-fire pecks. They are joined by a chestnut-sided warbler that must be fattening up for its impending journey north, back to the scrubby old fields and second-growth forests of southern Canada and New England.

Below us is a stand of *Pothomorphe* piper plants, succulent, erect treelets with dinner-plate-sized leaves that smell of licorice. Hidden in their tangle, a nightingale wren begins its song. Its whistle starts high and then drops lower, then up, now a shade away, following a slow, even cadence, setting up a pattern which seems to be random and new each time but which always follows the same jagged, jazzlike avoidance of melody.

At 8 a.m., the bird chorus begins to wane as the cicadas wax louder and shriller, proclaiming the time to pull on boots and move. Michael and I want to see different things, so we go our own ways. Two is always a crowd if you hope to see any wildlife or to take your time with your own particular fascinations. I look for treehoppers and other insects. Michael probably has a special bird or snake in mind.

The day yields little new in the way of treehoppers. But it hardly matters. I take pleasure in the spectacle created by the *Diospyros* persimmon trees, which now bear heavy crops of orange fruit. The abundance is too much for the ungainly crested guans, birds the size of turkeys that thrash about, dislodging fruit as they forage. Below one tree, a mass of fallen fruit ferments; I find six large, iridescent blue butterfly wings and guess that a passing jacamar has taken unfair advantage of the fruit-drunk Morphos.

By noon, the river beckons. The rushing water pauses and eddies here and there in clear, deep pools tinted pale blue. It is cool enough to dispel any sense of midday torpor. Along the banks is an unfamiliar plant, a member of the same family as coffee, with a creamy white, 10-centimetre-long, trumpet-shaped flower that ends in a mandala of wavy petals and exudes a scent of jasmine. Huge black carpenter bees buzz in red melastoma flowers the size of roses. A white hawk, a ghostly bird that haunts the dark edge of the forest, perches unobtrusively on a limb, patiently watching for a snake to risk a sunbath.

The diversity and beauty of tropical rainforest incorporate the garish, the ornate and the intricate. The scarlet macaw (*Ara macao*), left, typifies the brilliance of tropical bird life; the passion flower (*Passiflora pittieri*), centre, evokes the rainforest's unique floral forms; and the pupa of the passion-vine butterfly (*Heliconius hewitsoni*), right, suggest elegance.

11

The protected rainforests of the Monteverde Cloud Forest Reserve support some of Costa Rica's 850 species of bird, 700 species of butterfly and 200 species of mammal. But there is a constant tension between modern industrial and agricultural programmes and habitat preservation.

At around 4 o'clock in the afternoon, the band-backed wrens begin again to chatter and scold. A flock of chestnut-headed oropendolas, highly social relatives of orioles, stages a concert in black and yellow, wheeling and circling through the clearing below the cabin, calling noisily. Soon, they settle on a tree crown and embark on an extended, more intimate dialogue with distinctive liquid songs that sound like gurgling, dripping water. These are the sounds of social interaction, the greetings of one's own kind, and they mark the time for me to return, to sit once more on the bench admiring the sweep of the landscape after the confines of the forest. As always, we commemorate the day with an aromatic drink or two of rum.

Below us, the humid breath of untold billions of leaves begins to cool and condense. From the forest, a spotted woodcreeper calls. Its sinking, mournful notes express the mood — the unspeakable sadness of mist and cloud gathering soft and grey on the thickly forested hills, of dusk settling down the valley as it has done for countless days and years. Away on the farthest northeastern ridge, we can see a swath of pasture, the frayed edge of this island of forest.

Almost every reflective moment of a day like this in Peñas Blancas is attended by a mixture of hope and trepidation. A few years ago, chain saws were busy felling the trees, converting the valley into sodden, unproductive pasture. Now, as the result of a joint conservation effort by Costa Ricans and people from the United States, Canada and Europe, much of the forest is protected. The wildlife is bouncing back after decades of hunting: the collared peccary population is growing; hard on its heels is the burgeoning cat population. More support is pouring in to maintain this watershed. The entire country is counting on these forests to capture and regulate the flow of water into its Lake Arenal hydroelectric system, a billion-dollar installation that generates half of Costa Rica's electricity and much of its irrigation water. But just beyond the reserve, deforestation proceeds, driven by the combined forces of human population growth and poorly planned — or unplanned — economic development.

I know the family of the man cutting that distant ridge. A generation ago, the patriarch, a landless *campesino*, rode into these mountains on a makeshift trail. With his wife, he produced 20 children, all of them still living, all of them married, all with children of their own. Their family reunion could fill a village. In this family, too, I have seen the mix of optimism and apprehension that surrounds tropical conservation. The brother of the man clearing the pasture on the ridge once worked for me cutting trails. Before that, he felled more than his share of the Arenal Forest Reserve. He moved on to capitalize on the ecotourism trade that the nearby Monteverde Cloud Forest Reserve has created and now makes a much better living by renting horses and guiding tourists. He has two children, and that is plenty, he says. These are hopeful signs. But I can remember a trip we made not long ago to the other side of this valley. As we stood overlooking the watershed above Lake Arenal, I commented that there was still a lot of forest on these slopes. "Too much," he replied. "Too much."

Although he makes his living from the tourist traffic to the forest reserve and gets his electricity from its runoff, my friend grew up believing that pasture is progress, that untouched forest is a sign of underdevelopment and rural poverty. His is not an isolated, backwater mentality but the same prevailing belief that guides the urbane and powerful politicians, economists, bankers and religious leaders and informs the agricultural, industrial and urban cultures they direct. The leaders of modern society are well educated in the liberal arts, in economics, in technology. But what value do they place on the woodcreeper's lament or on the *Sobralia*, which bloom for a single day and can never be bought or sold?

Long ago, conservationist Aldo Leopold observed that the land-use practices which resulted in habitat destruction were the consequence of economics. He also argued that "economic laws may be permanent, but their impact reflects what people want, which in turn reflects what they know and what they are." This book seeks, in a small way, to change what people know and what they want. Communicating something of the intricate beauty of the rainforest will not be enough to guarantee its survival. But it is part of the incremental process of altering the human understanding and appreciation of nature. All the other components — institution-building, debt reduction, aid for sustainable development, improved planning, scientific research — necessary to make the preservation of tropical forest technically and materially possible will not

be enough if an interest in nature does not exist in the hearts and minds of people.

Any sketch of a subject so profoundly diverse, created with a few thousand words and a few hundred photographs, must give a biased view. In this book, we confine most of our material to the New World Tropics, with special emphasis on Costa Rica and Peru, where we have spent most of our time recently. We confess — without apology — to being anecdotal and speculative; these activities are a large part of the enjoyment of tropical natural history. But we also attempt to cover some classic themes that have long fascinated tropical biologists: the importance of diversity, mimicry, the wealth of species and nutrient cycles. Some of the chapters are oriented toward specific organisms: the sloths so specialized for life in the treetops; the snakes that haunt the thoughts of rainforest residents and visitors alike. Other chapters try to trace ecological connections and patterns. Comparisons with the temperate zone are made for a reason: The fate of these unique tropical habitats depends on the will and resources of people from both North and South.

We have tried to proselytize by bringing words and images together in a portrait of the rainforest. If we could, we would bring the sounds, the tastes, the textures and the smells as well. But perhaps it is better that you acquire these for yourself.

A.F., Peñas Blancas, Costa Rica, March 1989

Entire populations of *Sobralia* orchids growing in the rainforest canopy open their large snow-white blossoms in unison. But the fragile blossoms survive for only a single day.

ROOTS
OF DIVERSITY

THE ORIGINS
OF TROPICAL VARIETY

As the Rio Manú percolates through the eastern foothills of the Peruvian Andes, it comes to resemble a giant stream of *cafe con leche*. Carrying a surprising burden of suspended silt and sand as it wends its way toward the Amazon, the Manú both erodes and builds the floodplain. The current carves away the bank on the river's outward curves and lays down beaches on its inward curves. These beaches come and go, disappearing under the muddy flood during the rains and emerging once more during dry season.

In August, when the new crop of sugar-sand beaches stands high and sunbaked, a handsome and instructive set of birds begins to nest. Sand-coloured nighthawks insert their cryptically mottled selves among the boldly patterned black skimmers and cool white terns. Orinoco geese bare their russet-orange chests. There is an ecological familiarity to this association of birds that any temperate-zone naturalist will recognize, and it offers an interesting contrast to the adjacent forest.

Each bird in this decidedly tropical place seems to be an ecological replica of a temperate-zone counterpart. Swallows much like northern tree swallows nest in the emergent skeletons of drowned trees, foraging back and forth above the river and gleaning, as swallows do everywhere, the invisible drift of tiny insects. A cocoi heron, with the size and regal demeanour of the northern great blue heron but tailored in elegant grey with black and white calligraphy on its chest, stalks the shallows, always alone. More sociable sandpipers take smaller fry. And just as they do along the Eastern Seaboard, the black skimmers doze in full sun. They leave it to the kingfishers to dive for the fish that stay low by day. The skimmers begin to glide in the soft light of dusk and carry on by the light of the moon and stars, using their elongated, protruding lower bills to chisel up small fish dawdling at the surface. Geese browse the succulent sprouts greening the new edge of the landscape.

The birds on the beaches of Manú employ the same feeding behaviours as birds on the sandy shores of the more extreme latitudes of the northern hemisphere. The terns here are just as pugnaciously defensive as they are everywhere, rising up noisily at your approach and swooping just above your head so that you feel the breath of their angry wings. A yellow-billed tern hovers above the water, a beating band of light like a letter M dancing against the green backdrop of trees; then it twists head down and lifts its wings to set off the vertical plunge. It emerges with a silver minnow held sideways in its pastel yellow bill.

In all these aspects, the community of birds along the beaches of the Manú seems comparable to the bird community one might find sharing a beach on, for example, Cape Cod. To be sure, there are a few exclusively tropical niceties on Manú's beaches, such as the bizarre horned screamers with their ornamented heads. Yet even they waddle in pairs and feed much like geese. For the most part, this tropical habitat supports a bird community close to that of its temperate counterpart.

Once you step into the forest, however, the apparent similarities vanish. The number of bird species and the richness of their behaviours take on uniquely tropical dimensions. There are more breeding birds in Amazonian rainforest than in any other place on Earth. If we total up the numbers of breeding bird species in different parts of the globe, we see that Amazonia is the end point of a trend in which species richness accelerates as we approach the equator from north or south. If we compare areas of roughly the same size, Greenland rings in with 56 breeding species, Labrador 81, Newfoundland 118, New York State 195, Guatemala 469, Panama 1,100 and Colombia 1,395.

In this regard, birds are not exceptional. Most terrestrial life forms increase in species diversity as one moves from higher latitudes toward the equator. I can collect hundreds of butterflies in the fields and forests around my Ontario residence in a day, but my collection might embrace only a few dozen species. Manú probably holds 1,000 species. A recent count done in an Amazonian rainforest found 283 tree species in a single hectare. For comparison, there are few natural forests in temperate zones where one could find more than a couple of dozen tree

Epiphytic plants such as the orchid (*Huntleya meleagris*), left, bromeliads and vines are important contributors to tropical diversity. The water-filled bromeliad (*Nidularium* spp), centre, supports aquatic animals. The sticky glandular secretions of the blue passion flower (*Passiflora foetida*), right, are adaptations that select for specialized pollinators and defend the plant against grazing insects.

species per hectare. Animal-diversity differences are even greater. For example, on one individual tree from the area just south of Manú, a collection of ants identified by biologist E.O. Wilson yielded 43 species, more than occur in all of the British Isles. Perhaps the most fundamental challenge of tropical ecology is to account for this bewildering diversity, the ecological and genetic variety that is the hallmark and glory of tropical rainforest.

Leading into the forest from one of the beaches along the Manú is a transect trail where ecologists and ornithologists such as John Terborgh, John Fitzpatrick, Charles Munn, Scott Robinson and assorted colleagues have recorded more than 500 bird species. The trail slices through the successional sequence that is left as the riverbed winds across the alluvial plain. One abruptly passes from pure sun beating on a low monoculture of sunflowers that springs up on the virgin sand into the sudden shade created by a wall of giant *Gynerium* cane, which itself fades into stands of lush heliconia and ginger.

Figs and other weedy pioneer trees dominate the next successional phase, and then the trail moves into the upland forest above the floodplain. Where the most diverse temperate forest might support 40 bird species, the same area of forest along the Manú supports six times as many.

Ecological diversity proliferates in the forest. In addition to more widespread sorts of birds such as flycatchers, vireos, tanagers, woodpeckers, warblers, pigeons and the like, the birder will meet leaftossers, toucans, motmots, tinamous, manakins, macaws, nunbirds, antbirds, becards, trumpeters, giant ground-cuckoos—birds that have no ecological counterparts in northern forests.

Before any ecological explanation of the state of the world is given, caveats are in order: history and geography play a role in influencing diversity. By a quirk of evolutionary fate, bromeliads—for example, the pineapple family of some 2,000 species—flourish only in Neotropical rainforest, having never evolved or established themselves in Africa and Asia. The forests there are no doubt the poorer for it. Floras and faunas from North America and South America are still mingling as a result of the emergence of the Panamanian land bridge millions of years ago. Something of a region's variety will be owing to the history of such an exchange. Speciation rates are influenced by geography—areas such as the Andean foothills are extraordinarily rich in endemic species, and their generation may cause Ecuadoran rainforests to have greater diversity than more distant Brazilian forests. Of the larger, slower evolutionary processes, we have but an inkling. It is easier to look at ecological correlations of diversity.

John Terborgh has tried to answer the question, What ecological factors allow so many bird species to share an Amazonian rainforest? The beaches where his Manú transect begins provide a revealing starting point for a temperate-tropical comparison.

The absence of any profound difference in the temperate and tropical bird communities found on a beach is a result of a fundamental physical and ecological similarity in the habitats. This habitat provides only a simple two-dimensional nesting surface and a volume of water in which to feed. In both places, the birds have essentially the same limited spectrum of resources to divide up. By contrast, temperate and tropical forests, although superficially alike in being composed of large trees, offer a radically different spectrum of resources.

Ornithologists pay much attention to food resources and with good reason. Being small, warm-blooded organisms, birds spend a great deal of their day hunting for food; indeed, studies show that competition for food and for territories which contain food is a dominant feature of avian life. It is not surprising, then, that food diversity is a key to tropical bird diversity. Tropical rainforest offers food resources not found in temperate forests. For example, a large number of tropical-forest birds are specialized followers of army ants; a great radiation of antbirds, ovenbirds and woodcreepers gleans the insects stirred up by army-ant raids. Although some army ants make it into the temperate zones, they are exclusively subterranean and so offer no such opportunity for temperate-forest birds.

Many tropical birds are frugivores that take advantage of the year-round occurrence of fruit in tropical forests. Such a resource is available only at certain times in temperate forests—and in dry tropical habitats, for that matter—and thus only in tropical rainforest is there a great proliferation of frugivores such as cotingids. Terborgh compared Manú's avifauna with that of a prime hardwood forest in South Carolina, one of the richest forests left in the temperate zone. Of the 40 species breeding in that temperate forest, only 7 species included sig-

nificant amounts of fruit and nectar in their diet. In Manú, 84 species make use of fruit and nectar.

Dead leaves are another resource that has a uniquely tropical importance. They are always present in rainforest and act as hideouts for many insects. Accordingly, there is a guild of birds in tropical forests that always searches in dead leaves. No temperate birds use this technique as their primary food-foraging behaviour.

In fact, none of the foregoing life-history options are available in the temperate zone. But when Terborgh toted up the contribution of these tropical foraging strategies, he found that they account for only about one-third of the increased forest-bird diversity in the Tropics.

Another 17 percent of Manú's avian diversity is due to birds that specialize in feeding on large insects. In both temperate-zone forests and the Tropics, the majority of birds are insectivores, at least when they are breeding. But in contrast to temperate insectivores, many tropical birds such as motmots and nunbirds are specialized predators of small vertebrate animals and huge insects like katydids. I once watched a motmot swoop down to grab a *Dichotomius* dung scarab, a beetle so strong that it is virtually impossible to hold in one's fist because it burrows and claws its way through one's fingers. The beetle is nearly the size of a walnut, and its layers of corrugated black chitin make it almost as heavily armoured. The motmot picked up the beetle with its heavy, forcepslike, slightly serrated bill, flew up to its stout perch and vigorously smacked the beetle up and down and back and forth on the limb until it was thoroughly tenderized. I could hear the beetle cracking under the bludgeoning force. Temperate insectivores simply do not do that sort of thing. A turkey's crushing gizzard might be up to tackling such an item, but few other temperate-forest birds could handle it. And unlike turkeys, motmots are able to swoop down on terrestrial crabs and to snag lizards, especially anole lizards, from tree trunks. In short, tropical birds such as motmots, anis and nunbirds consume prey items in a size range that is largely absent from the temperate woods.

Half the diversity of Manú's forest avifauna appears to exist simply by virtue of greater ecological specialization. The subdivision of physical space is an obvious factor in packing species together in ecological communities. Bird species are often ecologically separated by search-and-capture behaviours that, in turn, are related to the structure of the vegetation where they occur. Robert MacArthur, a founder of the study of community ecology, showed that structure in the forest environment is an important contributor to diversity. Some birds forage in the tree crowns, some in the midstrata and others in the understorey or on the ground. Certainly, a tall rainforest offers more height than does a temperate hardwood forest. But no one who studies tropical birds, including Terborgh, believes that the height of the trees accounts

Most temperate-zone orchids grow on the ground, but in the Tropics, tens of thousands of orchid species, including these *Cattleya skinneri*, Costa Rica's national flower, grow as epiphytes. High levels of humidity and rainfall as well as freedom from frost allow epiphytes to flourish in the rainforest.

17

A scintillant hummingbird (*Selasphorus scintilla*) feeds at an epiphytic blueberry (*Vaccinium poasanum*), right. In rainforest and cloud forest, many species of blueberry are found growing high above the ground in the canopy, where they provide a year-round supply of nectar for hummingbirds. Likewise, the rich assemblies of bromeliads and other epiphytes, far right, serve as foraging sites for insects and in turn for insectivorous birds.

for most of the ecological segregation in rainforest.

To my mind, far more important than mere height is the fact that tropical rainforest trees can support epiphytes — plants which grow on other plants, which are freed from the need to connect with the earth and which grow in shapes and locations unused by temperate plants. Lianas rise from the forest floor, free-swinging like twisted ship's cables, until they grasp a limb and begin to run laterally through the canopy. Stringier vines plaster their leaves against the trunk. Inspection of their leaves reveals algae, lichens and mosses. Clusters of ferns, dangling cacti, carpets of heathlike shrubs and small trees wholly lacking contact with the soil can be seen on the bole and limbs of the tree.

After spending any time in the Tropics, you tend to take the vegetation for granted. But when you return to the temperate forest, you are struck by its stark, nakedly aus-

tere characteristics. Coastal forests of the temperate zone may be hung and speckled with epiphytic mosses and lichens, but it is only in the Tropics that the higher plants begin colonizing, climbing and carpeting every solid surface, from tree buttresses and boles to limbs and leaves. It is the higher plant epiphytes which give tropical vegetation its exuberant appearance and which are a basic component of tropical diversity.

Epiphytes number some 30,000 species in 850 genera and 65 plant families. In tropical rainforest and cloud forest, epiphytes account for 34 to 63 percent of the total number of plant species. In cloud forest, epiphytes reach their full potential, making up 40 percent of the total plant biomass. Important plant families such as the orchids are primarily epiphytic, and they achieve this state only in the Tropics. All temperate-zone orchids are dependent on soil for a water supply to replenish the moisture lost during evapotranspiration. Yet in tropical rainforest, although orchids do grow on the ground, vastly more grow as epiphytes—20,000 species, according to one count. In their elevated niches, orchids assume a fantastic diversity of growth forms, from sprawling vines and dangling, ropelike strands to bushy clumps with massive leaves and compact, mossy growths that carpet the uppermost twisted, wind-raked tree limbs. A survey of a single tree in a Venezuelan rainforest revealed a community of 47 different species of epiphytic orchid.

What makes epiphytism possible on such a grand scale is the same thing that is responsible for the diversity of rainforests: a damp and invariably warm atmosphere. The argument is an old one and is probably too prosaically mechanical for most ecologists to find attractive. They have variously debated whether greater productivity, predation rates, evolutionary time, speciation rates, climatic stability and other forces have generated high tropical diversity. All of these may be factors, but the tropical diversity the naturalist encounters on the ground stems from a climate that makes it possible.

Tropical-plant growth forms like strangler figs are possible only where there is freedom from the physical damage of freezing. An infant strangler fig growing high above the forest floor in the crotch of a tree may dangle its pencil-thick roots 50 metres to the forest floor with no risk of ice exploding its delicate plumbing. Humidity makes things easier for leaves. In the midlevels of tropical rainforest, philodendron leaves the size of umbrellas grow on tree trunks, completely cut off from the soil. Northern aroids like jack-in-the-pulpit or skunk cabbage retain something of the lushly huge leaves of their tropical relatives, but they are confined to moist, almost marshy shade because of the rate at which their leaves transpire water. Compare rainforest cacti with desert cacti. In the driest deserts, cacti grow as spiny columns or barrels that trade off a reduced photosynthetic surface area for a well-defended, highly reflective barrier against water loss and overheating. Desert cacti must have root contact with soil in order to draw up a store of water during the periods of moisture. In rainforest, cacti are typically spine-free, and the stems can grow flattened out, leaflike, to intercept as much light as possible. They may send roots out from any stem section or have almost no roots at all simply because ambient moisture levels are so high.

It may be true that many tropical trees, especially those in the canopy, have the same unlobed oval leaf shape with a pronounced drip tip for shedding water. Yet the larger truth is that when all plants are considered, there is a fantastically greater array of leaf shapes and sizes in a tropical forest than in a temperate-zone forest. A rainforest's climatic constancy allows specialization and hence variety in design at all levels, from enzymes to gross architec-

ture. Although rainfall is often seasonal in the Tropics, other physical parameters are far more constant. At the equator, the maximum amount of sunlight in any day falls on the equinoxes, but that amount is only 13 percent greater than the minimum amount during the solstices. At temperate latitudes, say, 50 degrees, the difference between the minimum and maximum sunlight leaps to 400 percent. In the north, then, a plant must endure constantly changing day lengths, great temperature differences and a profound waxing and waning of its energy supply. The temperature difference between night and day in a tropical rainforest is as great as the variation in the entire year. In a temperate zone, the temperature will fluctuate from as hot or hotter than any tropical rainforest to well below freezing. Such climatic variations encourage conformity in design. In extremely windy areas, all trees reach the same reduced height. In areas where rainfall fluctuates greatly, diversity falls off sharply and plants exist in a limited set of shapes and sizes.

If this climatic argument is true, there should be not only a temperate-tropical diversity gradient but also a relationship between rainfall, seasonality and plant diversity in tropical forest. Botanist Al Gentry has surveyed plant-species counts for a number of tropical sites and found a strong correlation between rainfall and plant diversity. Wet forests were three times as diverse as dry forests, and moist forests were intermediate. Epiphyte diversity responded most strongly to rainfall, while lianas and large trees were little affected by changes in precipitation. The rate of increase is correspondingly greater for epiphytes, which is just what we would expect for plants that have no opportunity to draw on the great buffering reservoir of soil moisture.

Nor is it only plants that are offered more opportunities by a warm, rainy climate. Frogs are also freer in rainforest, and a wide range of climbing tree frogs uses water-filled tree holes and epiphytes for breeding and feeding. This, in turn, makes life possible for crane hawks, which have double-jointed knees that bend both forward and backward, allowing them to stick their legs into tree holes in search of prey.

Because there are insects that feed on the leaves of epiphytes and the collections of humus and detritus which gather around their roots, tropical birds have a wide range of places to forage. Many tropical birds subdivide the unique structures offered by epiphyte communities such as lianas, another fundamentally tropical-forest feature. A hectare may contain more than 1,000 liana stems, which reach into the canopy and stretch from one tree crown to another; the forest is literally woven together by their resilient climbing, clinging tendrils and stems. This growth form composes about 20 percent of the forest's biomass and has become a site of specialization. Vine searchers — the various foliage gleaners and other ovenbird species

—spend much of the time rummaging in their tangles.

Likewise, large radiations of climbing lizards such as anoles and geckos have followed their insect prey into the trees. Herpetologist Alan Pounds has studied montane-rainforest anole communities in Costa Rica and found that they, too, have subdivided the forest structurally. Some species are canopy-specialized, while others segregate at various levels of the understorey and at light gaps, such as those created by tree falls. Their body forms and movement patterns vary accordingly: there are runners, jumpers and crawlers, depending on the sort of vegetation and substrate on which they live.

That particular diversity argument should not hold for groups such as terrestrial mammals that would be little affected by structures beyond their reach. Indeed, ground-dwelling mammals show little of the sharp diversity increase that epiphytes, birds, insects and other organisms do as we approach the equator and move from dry to wet areas. Reinforcing this pattern is the fact that mammals such as bats, which can divide up the air space and tiers of the forest and which feed on the broader range of foods offered by the upper echelons of the forest, show the same sharp increase in species diversity as one moves from the temperate zone toward the equator. A study of rainforest in Queensland, Australia, concluded that it is the structure of the vegetation itself which determines the organization of the community of bats found in the for-

est. Bats react to the pockets of space in the forest mosaic. Species with broad, manoeuvrable wings occupy the dense canopy; others with faster flight and long, narrow wings work the open spaces.

Such diversity patterns also hold for monkeys and other arboreal mammals that forage in the upper levels of the forest. Structural features like vine tangles offer domiciles for monkeys such as the pygmy marmoset, which lives in family groups, sucks tree sap and retreats to the protective mazes when threatened. And the monkeys themselves support formidable birds such as harpy eagles and ornate hawk-eagles that are sit-and-wait predators of primates and other canopy mammals. They have no temperate-forest equivalent. This concatenation of diversity began with the climate and the plants that make arboreality possible.

It is not only the complex structure of the rainforest flora that is important. The larger significance of greater plant diversity is that each species opens additional means of subdividing the environment for shelter as well as for foraging sites. Over the years, the epiphytes build up a mat of humus on tree limbs that acts as a foraging ground for canopy specialists like ochraceous wrens, which root there for beetle and fly larvae. But the epiphytes also provide resources for a range of herbivorous insects such as leaf-mining flies and flower-eating caterpillars. The flowers supply nectar, oil and perfume for bees, flies,

Climbing vines, left, are a prominent feature of tropical forests, as are climbing arboreal animals. They include organisms like the barred leaf frog (*Phyllomedusa tomopterna*), above, that depend on high levels of rainfall and humidity in order to pursue a life above the ground.

Tropical rainforests are characterized by the great ecological specialization of many organisms such as this passion-vine butterfly (*Heliconius clysonimus*) pollinating a cucurbit vine (*Psiguria* spp). The vine provides sticky masses of pollen that are eaten by the butterfly as well as transferred to other flowers.

hummingbirds and butterflies. The fruits are eaten by birds and mammals.

Consider the tank bromeliads, which add both structural complexity and aquatic microhabitats to the upper echelons of the forest. Costa Rican biologist Claudio Picado surveyed the fauna found in tank bromeliads and toted up an amazing 250 species. In addition to a rich resident fauna of mosquitoes, midges and syrphid flies, tank bromeliads provide breeding sites for the spectacular giant damselfly. The damselfly feeds on the other insects and possibly on the tadpoles that live in the tanks. The adult has a 17-centimetre wingspan, which exceeds that of all other damselflies and enables the insect to specialize in hovering delicately in front of an orb-weaving spiderweb for an indelicate meal: it plucks out the spider and consumes its abdomen. But the most remarkable feature of this damselfly is the almost hallucinatory effect it creates when it is encountered in the forest. Its wings are transparent save for a bold dab of blue or yellow pigment on each wing tip, and its thin, dark body is virtually invisible. Its forewings and hind wings beat out of phase so that only the dancing spots of colour are seen bouncing back and forth as it moves slowly and mysteriously through the shady understorey.

In spite of the damselfly nymphs, *Dendrobates* frogs place their tadpoles (and other frogs lay their eggs) in bromeliads, a development that has led to tree frogs such as *Hyla zeteki* relying on the eggs of others as their primary food. Stretched-out lizards are found in bromeliads, and their body forms appear suited for reaching far down into the recessed crevices in search of insect larvae. Hummingbirds pollinate the bold inflorescences. Skipper butterfly caterpillars feed on bromeliad leaves, and in the Andes, spectacled bears pull down the leaves to eat the soft, blanched bases.

Bromeliads may be an exceptionally small ecosystem, but the net result of adding any plant to an ecosystem is the triggering of an ecological multiplier effect. In thus praising plants, we should not forget that adding an animal to an ecosystem allows for the same result. Every vertebrate in a tropical forest is host to an abundance of parasites. That is something you can observe firsthand, whether you want to or not. Most people initially experience the richness of tropical parasites in the form of a microbial assault on the digestive tract. But every once in a while, something more distinctly tropical establishes a foothold.

A couple of years ago, I went hiking in Costa Rica wearing rubber boots that were oversized and leaky besides. It was raining, and the trail was a mixture of muck and rock. Eventually, the ends of my smaller toes became blistered from the slogging. After a few days had passed, the blisters toughened, a protective callus formed and I forgot all about them. Some weeks later, I was back in

22

Ontario and noticed that all my toes had reverted to their normal state save the smallest one on my right foot. This little pinkie was still callused on the end and had a dull, hollow feel to it. I left it alone for a time, but when the condition persisted, I thought it wise to investigate. For my studies, I had in hand a sharp, clean pair of forceps but no particular expectations. I jabbed experimentally at the callused mass, and it erupted. A mass of creamy, pinkish yellow eggs, like fish roe, burst out of the skin and hung there inelegantly on the end of my toe. After a few shocked seconds of puzzlement and contemplation, a light went on in my head. "A toe flea," I exclaimed with a mixture of horror and satisfaction.

For years, I had read about the so-called niguas, chigoes and jiggers (not to be confused with chiggers). Jiggers gained notoriety by attacking the feet of the first explorers of Latin America, who duly recorded their travails for their many readers. I had finally experienced that famous flea. *Tunga penetrans* is specialized and can be picked up when one goes barefoot, especially in the light, sandy soils frequented by farm livestock such as pigs. Females of this flea burrow into mammals, especially pigs, rats and humans. Safely ensconced several millimetres below the hide, they tap into the bloodstream and begin growing an egg mass. They swell prodigiously, reaching the size of a pea before bursting the well-formed larval fleas out into the environment, where they pupate.

The toe flea exemplifies the multiplier effect associated with parasitism. Like all parasites, it is an extreme anatomical specialist and lives within or subsists on a single individual, so each host species can be used by many different parasites. A predator, by contrast, typically lives on many individuals drawn from several prey species and thus has to be a generalist. Parasites, then, are more diverse than their larger host organisms. Vertebrate predators in a tropical rainforest are not excessively richer than those in drier or more temperate habitats, but parasites are exceedingly rich. Ecologist Peter Price has estimated that half of all species on Earth are parasitic. Neotropical vertebrates, especially mammals and birds, all carry with them vast collections of specialized mites, ticks, lice and sucking wingless flies. Even the sleek-skinned snakes harbour an extensive collection of specialized ticks. Many primary parasites transmit secondary parasites that cause ailments like leishmaniasis, malaria and Chagas' disease. As with vertebrates, invertebrate animals also host a wealth of smaller parasites. Specialized fungi, for example, prey exclusively on insects. Thus for every animal added to an ecosystem, we can multiply the species diversity by this parasitism factor.

Parasites add more to an ecological system than just new names to the species list. The ecological interactions in which parasites participate are themselves a sort of resource that can influence the coexistence of species.

Conventionally, ecologists have considered resources like food, habitat and breeding sites when studying the coexistence of species. But ecological interactions such as parasitism, pollination, herbivory and seed dispersal can also mediate coexistence by promoting ecological specialization. How is it possible for six species of passion vine to share the same patch of rainforest? Some passion vines attract and support hummingbird pollinators; other species of *Passiflora* are pollinated by bees. The foliage of the different species varies in chemistry and in the types of caterpillars that are able to feed upon the leaves. The fruits range from small, grape-sized productions that are probably bird-dispersed to melon-sized fruits that attract relatively large mammals. The range of animal pollinators, fruit dispersers and herbivores makes possible the evolution and coexistence of a rich set of *Passiflora* species. In turn, the diversity of the plants may mediate the coexistence of competing pollinators or herbivores.

Studying the process of plant-animal coevolution is a considerable challenge, since it occurs over an evolutionary time scale. At best, we know that such interactions lead to the generation of further diversity. Hence the ecologists' aphorism "diversity begets diversity" proves true, but only when the climate is constantly wet and warm enough to begin the initial green proliferation and promote its continuation. I try to keep this in mind whenever I have a face full of rain.

The clouds and mists that create tropical rainforest and sustain its diverse life forms are themselves created by the forest. The evaporative transpiration of the trees and other plants is important in forming clouds and in maintaining the climatic patterns of forested regions.

FROGS

LIFE HISTORY STRATEGIES
IN RAINFOREST AMPHIBIANS

  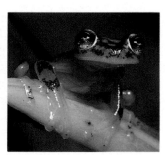

When two male poison arrow frogs stand upright, their arms wrapped around each other, their heads thrown back, calling out as they strain, stagger and wrestle on the forest floor, we are treated to an earnest display of machismo. Their skin is slick, their reddish yellow bellies are rotund, and their blue legs are bowed, causing a friend to liken them to sumo wrestlers in blue jeans.

One might say that the description of male *Dendrobates pumilio* frogs competing for breeding territories is anthropomorphic. I would agree. Let me immediately confess that my thoughts on frogs are coloured by empathy. Most naturalists feel the same way about frogs, perhaps because members of the order Anura—the "tailless ones"—are easy animals with which to identify. The great evolutionary biologists J.B.S. Haldane and Julian Huxley long ago observed: "The statement that frogs resemble men in any important degree may perhaps raise a smile. It is nevertheless true. We can recognize in the frog a great many parts that exist in ourselves, arranged, moreover, in the same way." That the frog is an organism which reminds us of ourselves may explain why so many cultures have myths featuring the conversion of frogs into princes, sorcerers and other sorts of humans. But more than simple anatomical kinship, it is also a question of attitude that makes frogs endearing.

Frogs, especially the tree frogs so common in rainforests, have a way of facing you with a goggle-eyed gaze that is disconcertingly humanoid. Their huge wrap-around mouths, while perhaps not actually resembling a smile, are certainly not frowning. Sitting hunched up as though in anticipation, they assume the posture and calm demeanour of patient listeners ready to participate in conversation.

Who cannot feel enchantment upon encountering the delicate translucence of a glass frog perched on a leaf, upon hearing the whooping entreaty of a pond full of male smoky jungle frogs (*Leptodactylus pentadactylus*) on a warm tropical evening or upon feeling the splayed sucker toes of a tree frog gently grasping one's skin? Our emotional responses to these appealing features of frogs are not irrelevant. The art of natural history lies in allowing such personal reactions to organisms to lead us into their biology.

Unlike most vertebrates, frogs tend to sit quietly rather than to panic and flee when you approach. That makes them an easy animal with which to make contact. Their moist skin has a tactile appeal and is tastefully patterned in perfect rainforest attire. And because they are virtually harmless, most species can be picked up with impunity; none that I know of stink up your hand the way many snakes and turtles do. Only a few of them bite with any conviction, and the small wounds they inflict are probably worth the novelty of being one of a handful of people who can claim to have been bitten by a frog. Their

sometimes potent defensive toxins are never injected. The giant toad *Bufo marinus* can squirt out a dilute stream of irritating toxin from its parotid glands, although to its credit, it does this more often to dogs than to humans. A few species such as *Leptodactylus pentadactylus* and *Phrynohyas venulosa* have a skin secretion that makes your fingers tingle or even burn if it gets into a wound; the exudates of certain species will induce vomiting if rubbed on your forearms (something various Guyanese tribes in search of a cathartic purification used to do willingly). Generally, however, for a frog to do you real damage, you have to chew it.

Even a cursory examination of these particular features of rainforest frogs reveals that two themes, moisture and predation pressure, explain the conspicuous and attractive aspects of their anatomy and behaviour. The humid rainforest microclimate has a liberating effect on frogs. A curious limitation of the physiology of these amphibians is a need for constantly high humidity. Yet in spite of their apparent affinity for the stuff, frogs never actually drink water. Instead, they drink and breathe through their skin. Water and respiratory gases pass freely back and forth across this huge membrane. In open or dry areas, frogs tend to stay in the water. But in rainforests, frogs sit openly on leaves. Temperate-zone frogs hop about using the same paired frog kick that jets them in bursts through the water. In rainforests,

The huge eyes of many rainforest frogs such as the red-eyed leaf frog (*Agalychnis callidryas*), left, and golden-eyed leaf frog (*A. annae*), centre, enable them to hunt at night. The transparent glass frog (*Centrolenella valerioi*), right, like the leaf frogs, avoids the bright tropical sun and is most active on wet, warm nights.

25

frogs with long, stretched-out limbs and digits, sometimes with webbed skin, climb arm over arm to their destination. The eyes are positioned forward on the head for better depth perception. The spider monkeys and flying squirrels of the amphibia, they are arboreal climbers that sometimes leap out into space and glide from one tree to another. By comparison, temperate-zone frogs seem a squat and lumpish lot.

The huddled posture that arboreal frogs typically adopt by tucking their limbs under their bodies is a water-conservation strategy which reduces evaporation from their surface area during dry times; it may also reduce heat loss. At room temperature and 100 percent humidity, a frog will lose only 20 percent of its metabolic heat through evaporative cooling; but if the humidity drops to only 94 percent, the heat lost through evaporation will equal all the heat generated by the frog's metabolism. A frog stretched out and placed in direct sun would wither away in no time; even the prodigiously large *Bufo marinus*, a 5-pin-bowling-ball-sized toad that can reach a weight of 1.2 kilograms and has a leathery, warty hide, is highly susceptible to water loss. At 80 percent humidity, an individual without water can become lethally dehydrated in 24 hours. Most frogs were made for warm, drizzly nights.

Access to higher nighttime humidity is one important benefit of being nocturnally active. But being active by night also helps the frog to avoid the legions of predators that are only too ready to make a meal of it. Fish have probably been eating frogs since ancestral frogs and fish began to diverge evolutionarily. Several species of snake have evolved into specialized hunters of adult frogs, and some bats have developed a sonar and hearing system that enables them to swoop down and snag calling males. Coatimundis, opossums — indeed, most carnivorous mammals — include frogs in their diet, as do many birds such as hawks, herons, rails, muscovy ducks and motmots. Crabs, spiders, water bugs and the larvae of some beetles and flies also attack frogs successfully. There are even frogs that specialize in eating other frogs. And although certain tadpoles may be capable of chemical

defence, most can be slurped down expeditiously. Much of the radiation of rainforest frogs into new niches seems to be driven by these varied predation pressures.

The significance of predation on the life history of frogs is evident not only in their anatomy but also in their sophisticated reproductive behaviour. The battle of the male *Dendrobates pumilio*, performed so openly in broad daylight, on dry land and in such bold attire, might strike most naturalists as unusual. The scene arouses an initial interest similar to that evoked by witnessing a barroom brawl. But it is not long before we start to wonder exactly why the frogs are fighting on the forest floor, so far from any river or pond. What sort of pay-off do they receive for their efforts?

The reproductive and parental rituals of *Dendrobates* are among the most elaborate in nature. The male defends areas of leaf litter in a patch of forest where there are also water-filled bromeliads that provide a habitat for the tadpoles. He advertises with a buzzy, chirping call that attracts females. When a female approaches, the territorial male hops to a leaf and deposits a squirt of sperm, upon which the female lays 3 to 10 relatively large eggs. The male then broods the eggs right on the forest floor. After about two weeks, the eggs hatch into tadpoles that wriggle up onto the back of the female and adhere with the aid of their mucous coating and sucking mouths. The adult frogs then carry and distribute the tadpoles among

Male strawberry poison dart frogs (*Dendrobates pumilio*), left, wrestle on the forest floor for control over territory; their bold colours advertise their toxicity to would-be predators. The rear-fanged snake (*Pliocercus euryzonus*), above, just one of many snakes that specialize in a diet of frogs, is in the process of swallowing a rain frog (*Eleutherodactylus noblei*).

27

the territory's water-filled bromeliads. The bromeliads contain some food for the tadpoles, but to ensure an adequate supply, the tadpoles are usually dispersed one per plant. More remarkably, the female repeatedly visits the plants to lay unfertilized eggs in each one. The tadpoles puncture the eggs and suck out their yolky contents.

Territory-holding male *Dendrobates* are evidently a limited resource and one that females court actively; studies of breeding areas have found that female adults usually outnumber males. In species where the male broods eggs or carries tadpoles, the female takes a particularly aggressive role in courtship. In the case of *Dendrobates auratus*, a beautiful species with blue-green, turquoise and dark markings, the female makes an attempt to gain a male's attention by leaping on his back and poking him with her forelimbs.

The long, thin, delicate limbs of the emerald tree frog (*Hyla musica*), above, are a typical adaptation for climbing about the vegetation. A pair of reticulated glass frogs (*Centrolenella valerioi*), right, tends two clutches of eggs laid on a leaf overhanging a forest stream, preventing the eggs from drying out and guarding them against egg parasites and small predatory insects.

An adult *Dendrobates* is freed somewhat from the threat of predation by virtue of its alkaloid-impregnated skin, although specialized predators such as *Leimadophis* snakes will eat even the most toxic frogs, including *Dendrobates*. But this relative immunity is only one factor that allows *Dendrobates* to wrestle and court by day.

The second significant aspect of *Dendrobates* breeding is that much of it takes place on land. The humid rainforest microclimate and the many small, moist havens found there explain much of the reproductive variety frogs achieve in tropical rainforest. Herpetologist Martha Crump found 81 species of frog in one patch of Ecuadoran rainforest. Ecuador, incidentally, a tiny but fantastically varied country, has some 300 frog species. By comparison, Great Britain has but three, and the entire United States, with all its lakes, rivers and wetlands, has only 80 species.

The low anuran diversity in North America is initially surprising; a temperate-zone naturalist might reasonably expect lakes, ponds and marshes to be the most popular haunts of frogs. It is not true. Preferred habitats are, in fact, those harbouring the fewest predators. The frog diversity in the main Amazonian rivers, for example, is as low as the fish diversity is great. Instead, most frogs occur in the forest proper.

A tropical rainforest offers a variety of habitats that no pond, lake or river can match. It is replete with small temporary ponds, such as water-filled bromeliads, tree crotches and holes. The latter are apparently defended by the male of the giant tree frog *Hyla miliaria*, which has

The huge throat sac of this calling male *Hyla severa* tree frog, above, is a resonating chamber. It amplifies a mating call designed to attract females and to repel male rivals. Like most frog species found in Costa Rican cloud forest, lemur frogs (*Phyllomedusa lemur*), right, are relatively well camouflaged, a reflection of the fact that many predators, among them various species of bird, monkey, bat and snake, include frogs in their diet.

Some songs are based on one note, others on clusters of notes. A number of frog species sing in synchronized choruses that may attract females while making it difficult for predators to home in on a specific target.

Frogs generate sound by means of inflatable air sacs, located under and alongside the mouth or body, that act as resonating chambers when air from the lungs and huge mouth cavity is blown across the vocal cords. Because of all their volume — sometimes as much as 100 decibels — it is often easier to hear rainforest frogs than to see them. A thumbnail-sized species of *Eleutherodactylus* known as the tink frog is particularly frustrating; its call is both loud and pervasive. As daylight fades in the cloud forest, a mounting chorus of "tink, tink, tink" — a penetrating staccato call — rings all around you. But try to find the callers. You bend your head this way and that, peering and trying to discern the nearest source. If you are absolutely still, one may start to call right beside you; as you inch toward it, however, the hidden caller becomes silent. The vociferous but tiny tink frog is rarely seen except by accident. This secretive aspect of frogs is sometimes well developed because various predators — bats, caimans, mammals and other frogs, especially the large engulfers such as *Bufo marinus* and *Leptodactylus pentadactylus* — are alert to frog calls.

The panoply of frog calls enlivens the rainforest during its darkest, dampest moments. On a drizzling,

dripping-wet evening, you will almost certainly hear them at their most enthusiastic. On a ridge top far from any pond or stream, there will be frogs of some sort; their most reliable characteristic is their ubiquity. Tree frogs will sit openly on the leaves of the shrubbery. You can stare into their large, gold-rimmed eyes without stooping, and they may make a chameleonlike change of colour in the light of your headlamp. You will find frogs clinging to tree trunks like bits of wet, rubbery lichen. As you sweep your headlamp along the trail, many a dull brown frog and sometimes a bold black, yellow and red *Atelopus* toad can be seen in the leaf litter, while far overhead in the treetops, a marsupial frog makes a barking sound.

The last time I went for a walk in a tropical forest, I was lucky. While inspecting a mass of blue flowers, I discovered that it held a tink frog. It perched cooperatively on my finger for a minute as I inspected it — a tiny, perfect bit of a frog; then an impressive two-metre leap carried it back into obscurity. I stood there for a few minutes, appreciating once more the particular pleasure frogs can provide. Having made their escape from the confinements of ponds and rivers, radiating into all the strata of the forest, rainforest frogs are a kind of zoological equivalent of epiphytic plants. They are an appropriate emblem of tropical rainforest, for they owe their rich diversity to the hallmark of that habitat. Freedom for frogs comes with the rain.

produces only a slight change in heartbeat in the opossum, and within half an hour, the animal shows no effect whatsoever. That adaptation enables the opossum to treat a swamp infested with rattlers and the related water moccasins and copperheads not as a health hazard but as a feeding opportunity. Interestingly, the opossum shows no resistance to cobra venom. That makes good evolutionary sense, since the Virginia opossum is naturally distributed in areas where rattlesnakes abound but cobras do not. Domestic cats, on the other hand, which evolved in the cobra-rich regions of Egypt, the Middle East and India, remain rather resistant to cobra venom.

The juvenile fer-de-lance (*Bothrops asper*), above, seen swallowing a rain frog (*Eleutherodactylus* spp), displays the flexible jaw apparatus that allows many snakes to swallow prey items greater than their own body weight. Vine snakes (*Oxybelis aeneus*), right, possess an extremely thin, elongate, green or brown body, a combination that provides camouflage while they hunt through tangled vegetation in search of anole lizards.

Similarly, mongooses are eight times more resistant to cobra venom than are rabbits, animals that have not coevolved with cobras.

Habitual snake-eating raptors such as white hawks and laughing falcons probably rely more on their heavily scaled legs than on an immunity to the poison to survive a venomous attack. To protect itself further, a laughing falcon, upon landing on a snake, will immediately bite off its prey's head. Nevertheless, there is a record of a red-tailed hawk dying with a coral snake in its talons, exhibiting the typical symptoms of paralysis and evidence of having been bitten in the leg. That may explain why birds such as motmots, which feed on snakes and whose range closely overlaps that of coral snakes, reportedly avoid coral snakes instinctively and why so many snakes have a banding pattern similar to the coral snake's.

Snake-eating snakes such as king cobras, king snakes and indigo snakes are thought to be immune to many kinds of snake venom. That natural immunity is what allows snakes like the mussurana to specialize in a diet of other snakes, including the highly toxic fer-de-lance. Such a specialization makes the mussurana one of the few snakes to be cherished by *campesinos* throughout Latin America.

As a rule, of course, snakes are not generally appreciated; people the world over wage war on them every chance they get, despite the fact that statistically, they have little to fear. But a heightened alertness and instinctive wariness occasioned by the knowledge that there are venomous snakes about will always remain part of the rainforest milieu. We can temper our ancient adaptive aversion with respect and with cautious admiration for a group of predators that has managed to make so much of such minimal equipment.

Yet A
one v
neo h
ing fe
peop
of co
open
ding
In th
rians
"do r
to th
sive
and t
to th
wart
pigs.
to ro
the s

Su
ple t
They
persa
than
pano
on th
in C

generally lack. In fact, a hunger for calcium may explain most of the reported cases of geophagy.

Calcium is especially limited in level areas of central Amazonia, where there is little erosive potential and subterranean forces have failed to bring new mineral-rich rock to the surface. Soils of white sand are especially infertile. Some idea of how nutrient-poor a habitat is and how effective is the nutrient sponging of the plants can be seen in the fertility of the runoff. Smaller streams and rivers in these areas have a characteristic black tint and calcium levels sometimes so low that analysts can get only a zero reading with their sophisticated equipment. In fact, plain rainwater contains twice as much calcium as does the river water, and what falls in the rain is obviously being retained very efficiently by the vegetation. The iron and aluminum content of the rivers is great, and their waters are, like peat bogs, highly acidic, with a pH of less than 4.5. One species of snail has traded the typical calcium-carbonate shell for one constructed mainly from a gluey secretion.

On land, the old, weathered upland soils are not seasonally inundated and are not enriched by silt. There, calcium levels also limit plant-growth rates. The behaviour of tropical tree roots is also an indicator of the importance of calcium. When bags of leaf litter are allowed to decay without contact between the litter and tree roots, various elements disappear at differing rates. Sodium, potassium and nitrogen leach away irrespective of root contact. But calcium and magnesium disappear much more quickly from a bag of litter with root contact than from one without. In effect, the roots mine the litter, sponging up the nutrients with great efficiency.

The absence of soil mineral salts such as calcium is one reason that clearing the forest and burning the slash to create cattle pastures is so unproductive; the bulk of the forest's fertility is held within the vegetation. Temperate soils may have a huge subterranean reservoir of fertile, nutrient-rich material, but in a tropical-forest system, as much as 95 percent of the fertile salts is held in the biomass of vegetation. When rainforest vegetation is cut and burned, the salts lie in a layer of grey ash on the surface of the soil. The first heavy rains leach away the ash, wasting most of the nutrient capital of this ecosystem.

The mineral salts that are left for the pasture plants are then exported at a great rate by agricultural harvesting. For example, each 1,000 kilograms of steer takes out of the system 27 kilograms of nitrogen, 7.5 kilograms of phosphorus and 13 kilograms of calcium. This degree of nutrient availability in a small area is simply not typical of tropical soils. A hundred hectares of forest that once contained thousands of tonnes of biomass and nutrients is required to sustain a single steer. If ever there were a case of making a pathetic molehill out of a magnificent mountain, this is it.

More than a century ago, Alfred Russel Wallace, travelling through Amazonia, encouraged the conversion. "I fearlessly assert," he wrote, "that here, the primeval forest can be converted into rich pastureland, into cultivated fields, gardens and orchards, containing every variety of produce, with half the labour and, what is more important, in less than half the time that would be required at home." Unfortunately, only the last element of his assertion has proved true. It is quick work to convert a complex forest into a simplified agricultural landscape, albeit an impoverished one. A couple of people armed with chain saws and matches can level and burn an astonishing amount of forest in a year. With a 60-tonne tree crusher, a single person can destroy 10 hectares every day.

The conversion of forest through felling and burning is often a one-way path that cannot easily be reversed by the successional process we are familiar with in temperate forests. After a forest fire in northern deciduous or coniferous forest, the vegetation surges back and the forest fills in rapidly. But in much of the Tropics, the nutrients lost when rains wash away the ash are unrecoverable. Even if the organic matter of a northern forest soil is lost during a fire, each winter freezing brings up mineral-rich rock and breaks it into soil. But the weathering of the parent material of the soil cannot replace the exported nutrients in most areas of the Tropics. Old soils have had all the nutrient salts taken out of them. Indeed, some studies have shown that the nutrients in tropical forest which are lost to leaching and runoff are replaced not so much as a result of the weathering of the bedrock and soil but from atmospheric input, dusts and dissolved material borne by wind and rain. It takes some 230 years of rain to replenish salts such as potassium.

Many tropical soils contain a high concentration of aluminum and low amounts of calcium. Sometimes, the aluminum is so concentrated that the soil becomes bauxite, from which aluminum can be commercially extracted. That concentration of aluminum and depletion of calcium is particularly taxing for most rainforest tree roots, since aluminum prevents them from functioning. The plants that seem best able to deal with the high-aluminum/low-calcium situation created by soil leaching are the weedy tropical grasses. As a matter of fact, vast areas of the Tropics in South America, New Guinea and Southeast Asia have been taken over by huge monocultures of tough, virtually inedible grasses. Though neither man nor beast gets any use from them, they persist in a perverse form of perpetual ecological revenge.

Tropical regions are not strangers to the calamity that follows the massive disruption of a nutrient cycle. The destruction of tropical soils, accelerated by the development of agriculture, may have been responsible for the demise of some great city states. Tikal, Angkor Wat and Palenque rose briefly in the midst of tropical forest and ended in ruins, thick with strangler figs. Some anthropologists believe that these cities exceeded the capacity of the surrounding land to supply their citizens with adequate food. Without efficient transport, it was impossible to import enough food to sustain the urban concentration of humans.

Yet in areas of poor tropical soils suitable only for growing rainforest, large cities are again growing up at a rapid rate. A few may someday become great and lovely, but most are so wretchedly out of balance with their surroundings that it is hard to imagine how they will ever escape the fate of Tikal and other similar civilizations. All of these cities are utterly dependent on the finite supply of currently cheap fossil fuels to transport their food from distant lands as well as to produce the fertilizer needed to replace the salts of the earth now being lost. The cleared areas of land around these cities are largely incapable of meeting the needs of the people living at present in the regions of tropical forest.

Year after year, for thousands of years before the conquest, Amazonia had supported perhaps five million people. The thinly spread rainforest tribes were able to live off the interest without destroying the nutrient principal of the soil. The salts of the earth, scarce though they were, were just enough to sustain the system. The present and growing masses of people who have replaced the rainforest societies with denser agricultural and urban developments exist only through massive imported subsidies of food and fertilizers. It is impossible even to speak of a nutrient cycle in such a system, since the term implies some kind of internal equilibrium.

Explorer John Stephens wrote of Palenque: "Nothing ever impressed me more forcibly than the spectacle of this once great and lovely city overturned, desolate and lost, discovered by accident, overgrown with trees for miles around and without even a name to distinguish it." Perhaps when the fossil fuels give up, fertilizer is not easily produced and the flow of food resources is stemmed, then the modern cities and pastures that have supplanted rainforest will likewise become overturned and ruined. But if there are still trees to crack the façades and open the cement with their calcium-hungry roots, still lianas to drape and soften the hard angular walls, still bromeliads and orchids to flower on window ledges and still macaws, peccaries and monkeys to reclaim their territory, the spectacle will be anything but desolate.

The great Mayan city of Palenque and its temples, above, may have been abandoned when local soils became too impoverished to grow enough food to support a large urban population. Because rainforest plants absorb nutrients so efficiently, rainforest streams and rivers, left, sometimes contain lower nutrient concentrations than does rainwater.

73

HERMITS & HELICONIAS

THE MICROCOSM OF PLANT & ANIMAL COEVOLUTION

Dropping down from the Atlantic side of the continental divide in central Costa Rica, the Peñas Blancas Valley is a gigantic slump of wet clay sprinkled with rock and slashed by mountain streams into slippery, knife-edge ridges and boulder-strewn ravines. The trail into the valley starts at the top with breadth and firmness, but in the centre of the valley, it begins to narrow as it moves up and down successive ridges. Eventually, it branches and meanders into a vague network that seems to have been expropriated from nimble-footed tapirs. The trails demand one's full attention. There are nettles to rebuke the careless. Gravity conspires with greasy mud, and even with concentrated footwork, there is an inevitable amount of slithering. In wet season, which lasts for 11 months, the mixture of horse traffic and rain stirs up a viscous slop that may suddenly suck a rubber boot right off your foot. One thoughtless step, and you are mired, wobbling on one leg like a drunken crane.

Under such conditions, it is not easy to watch for wildlife. Happily, however, there is a long stretch where the trail is flat enough to set one's feet on autopilot and let the senses wander. The ever present rumble of the river far below, the murmur of the feeder streams filtering through the mossy boles and tangles of vine and the green shade make daydreaming possible. It was on this stretch some years ago that I came face-to-face with my first hermit hummingbird.

Out of nowhere, it cut through my reverie with a salvo of indignant squeaks. It delivered its high-pitched message and then proceeded to spend the next few minutes inspecting me from various angles. Alternately, it approached and retreated, and as it hovered, it buzzed its wings loudly and flicked its long tail as though to call attention to its presence. I was able to admire at length the hermit hummingbird's bill, a tool gracefully but curiously curved, designed to weave one vital strand in a complicated web of ecological interactions. Then it darted away through the understorey.

Wildlife watching in rainforest is usually like this. The habitat does not offer panoramic spectacles. The words "tropical rainforest" may conjure up vistas populated by jaguars, brilliant macaws and flowers amidst the grandeur of towering buttressed trees. But the eager, expectant visitor is not regaled with the sight of charismatic vertebrates, gaudy birds and luminous orchids. In rainforest, close encounters with life that moves are usually rare but brilliant episodes; one is bedazzled for an instant and then left alone in the quiet greenery. Under such conditions, one must see the episode as part of a process; tracing the connections between organisms is the essence of rainforest appreciation.

There is a practical side to this approach that matches the habitat: you need hardly move your feet at all to go down many a long, convoluted ecological trail. If we follow the lead of the hermit hummingbird, it will take us directly to a spectacular, common and important group of rainforest plants, the heliconias. The association between the hermit and the heliconia is, like many natural interactions, not an obligatory tie but, rather, a loose mutualism. Its curving bill allows the hermit to drink at and pollinate the flowers of many heliconia species. In turn, the heliconias play a major part in making life possible for the hermit. The two organisms are conjoined in a classic case of tropical coevolution that also sustains a vast subsidiary of other rainforest organisms. In fact, if one wants to see truly representative rainforest wildlife, a patch of heliconias will serve as an ideal investigation site.

These members of the banana family (Musaceae) are among the most spectacular, abundant and accessible plants of the New World Tropics. Their bold, rhythmic forms seem drawn from a painting by Rousseau, and like Rousseau's flat, two-dimensional renditions of tropical vegetation, heliconias often stand in dense, regal walls along the edges of forests and riverbanks. Heliconias grow as clumps or as umbrellas composed of huge leaves shaped like long, drawn-out canoe paddles several metres in length. Quintessentially tropical, they can afford larger leaves than any cold- or dry-climate plants. The leaves of some species are glossed with a waxy, silvery sheen, while others wear a purple tinge underneath. Their yellow and

The extremely curved bill of the white-tipped sicklebill (*Eutoxeres aquila*), left, enables it to pollinate flowers such as *Heliconia reticulata*, whose deep, curved corolla and heavy flower bracts deny access to less specialized pollinators. A long, curved bill likewise enables the long-tailed hermit (*Phaethornis superciliosus*) to pollinate *H. irrasa*, centre. The same hermit at the scarlet passion flower (*Passiflora vitifolia*), right, will receive pollen on a different part of its head.

Heliconia trichocarpa has a dangling inflorescence and curved flowers that allow access only to hummingbirds such as the long-tailed hermits (*Phaethornis superciliosus*) with long, curving bills. This minimizes waste of both pollen and nectar on less specialized pollinators.

red flower bracts have a rigid, almost plastic solidity and a lively zigzag geometry and may reach lengths of two metres, dangling in bold pendants. Some inflorescences erupt as heavy columns from the base of the plant; others stand erect in spiky fountains of colour amid the greenery. The floral displays are designed to attract hummingbirds, and in lowland rainforest, if one wishes to watch these birds, finding a clump of heliconias is the best bet. Simply sitting nearby early in the day will be more rewarding than any amount of hiking.

The wedding of hummingbirds and heliconias is based on sex and energy. Like most plants, heliconias face the problem of transporting genes to and from other rooted individuals, but they require especially precise vectors for their pollen. Heliconias thrive where water and light are available to fuel their massive photosynthetic surfaces. In undisturbed forest, they are clustered in patches of light left by tree falls, along stream banks and in seasonally flooded habitat. Broadcasting their pollen on the wind or using casual insect visitors is not an effective way to move their genes to other heliconias because of their habitat preferences and patchy distribution. A hummingbird is ideal for such long-distance pollen transfer.

There is a reciprocity between hummer and flower, a matching of form and function that is satisfying to behold. Like all birds, the hummingbird sees reds and other colours that insects do not perceive. The heliconia's bracts stand out like a bright flag against the green; they house the tubular corollas that only the long bill of a hummingbird can negotiate. In order to meet the energy requirements of its heat-radiating body, the hummingbird must daily drink up to eight times its body weight in nectar, of which heliconias produce a copious supply. As the hummingbird drinks from the well of nectar the plant holds at its base, one of two things happens. Either the bird's bill or forehead is smeared with pollen from the plant's anthers, or the plant receives a fertilizing pollen load on its stigma from the laden bird.

The heliconia offers none of the sweet fragrance that lures bees and other insects to some flowers. In any case, like most birds', the hummingbird's sense of smell has atrophied. The heliconia's lack of scent and the elongated shape of its flower serve to exclude the swarms of unspecialized and less efficient insect pollinators. Many insects are catholic patrons of flowers and will visit dozens of different species, but the visit of a generalist pollinator has several disadvantages for a plant. An insect caked with flower pollen collected from half a dozen different species might clog the receptive stigma of the heliconia flower with useless types of pollen. A lack of selectivity by the flower visitor also means that any heliconia pollen the pollinator carries away may be likewise wasted in transfers to non-heliconias. In self-defence, the heliconia has evolved a flower that excludes such casual was-

trels from its nectar, an energy-rich resource that is expensive to produce.

This exclusionary targeting is further enhanced by the fact that the pollen of most heliconia species is placed on a particular part of the hummingbird. As many as a dozen heliconia species may occur in one area, and an individual hummingbird might visit several during a single foraging bout. The anthers of each heliconia species have a particular length or contortion which ensures that the pollen adheres to a unique spot on the visitor's bill or face.

Most heliconias produce only a few open flowers per morning, and each flower lasts just one day, requiring the hummingbird to move from plant to plant. It is interesting to note that heliconias produce a surge of nectar just at the dim, cool hour of daybreak, when insects are quiescent but hummingbirds are making their rounds. That is the time to witness the actual match of bird to flower, the brief blur and buzz of wings, followed by silence.

The high metabolism of hummingbirds may also be important in allowing heliconias to climb mountains. I have always been impressed by the similarity in growth form between a marantaceous plant known as *Calathea insignis* and certain heliconias. Calatheas, which also grow in clumps and have large, paddle-shaped leaves, produce a conspicuous column of yellow flower bracts. At first glance, many people mistake them for heliconias. In Monteverde, Costa Rica, the two grow side by side on the lower slopes of the mountain. But as one climbs to 1,500 metres and beyond, the calatheas attenuate and the heliconias persist in abundance. I suspect the difference is that the heliconia enjoys a partnership with hummingbirds, while the calathea depends on bees for pollination. In the lowlands, the calathea is pollinated by a diversity of orchid bees, but at higher elevations, only a couple of species of large bee pollinate it, no doubt because only large bees are able to thermoregulate and fly at low tempera-

Short-billed species such as the red-footed plumeleteer (*Chalybura urochrysia*) forage at and defend flowers that are better suited to the shape of their bills than are the more inaccessible heliconias.

77

A complex miniature ecosystem, heliconias serve a function for many rainforest species. Grazing insects feed on the leaves (*Heliconia irrasa*) and attract predators such as the green anole lizard (*Norops biporcatus*) by day, left. The barred leaf frog (*Phyllomedusa tomopterna*), above, visits an *H. stricta* by night. The flower bracts sustain aquatic invertebrate communities, and the flowers and fruits attract birds.

tures. Hermits drop out at high-altitude cloud forest, but other hummingbirds have developed the hermit's form and foraging strategy; indeed, some sort of hummingbird can be found at all elevations in Costa Rica. Perhaps that is why heliconias extend nearly 1,000 metres higher than do calatheas. (A calathea that does occur above 2,000 metres in the Colombian Andes has evidently become modified for pollination by the hummingbird.)

Heliconia species (*Heliconia wagneriana*) that have upright bracts often house small aquatic communities with dense populations of insects. The mosquito larvae feed on the populations of bacteria and small plankton that live in the water. The breathing tubes of syrphid fly maggots reach up from the bottom sediments where they feed.

These musings about hummingbird-assisted mountain climbing are speculation rather than scientific fact. But speculation is where the fun is, and much of the pleasure of standing by the heliconias watching a hummingbird blur and vanish is in imagining and wondering about the history and interlocked fates of plants and animals.

Other observations are much more verifiable. It is obvious that hermits are uniquely qualified to pollinate many heliconia species. Simply look inside the bracts, and you will find the curved flower tubes that cater exclusively to hermits. There is no substitute. Hermits offer more than just the right bill shape; they also have a foraging strategy that is conducive to this partnership. Unlike many short-billed hummingbirds, they do not defend a patch of flowers that they visit repeatedly. Hermits "trapline," moving from one clump of flowers to another, covering a circuit that may run for a kilometre or more through the forest. This means that hermits move pollen great distances with every foraging expedition.

Not aggressively territorial, hermits are easily displaced by other hummingbirds in contests over nectar sources. Ornithologist Gary Stiles points out that among non-hermits, control over a resource is usually size-related, with large hummers excluding smaller species. But even relatively large hermits are driven off by smaller, more aggressive non-hermits. The hermits survive because their unique curved bills allow them to exploit the specialized

heliconia flowers that their straight-billed competitors are denied.

Such dependence may go back to the very origins of the heliconia. Not all heliconias are pollinated by hermits. Sometimes, non-hermit hummingbirds visit the shorter-flowered species. However, Stiles suggests that the non-hermit heliconias are more recent innovations. He points out that the geographic distribution of hermits and heliconias is closely matched and that the two organisms appear to share an ancient coevolutionary history.

Over time, such relationships act as resources that other organisms evolve to exploit. A number of hummingbird flower mites, all members of the family Ascidae, use hummingbird bills to carry them from one flower to another, where they breed and feed on nectar and pollen. The mites, too, bear witness to the evolutionary impact of the long hummingbird bill. Ecologist Rob Colwell notes that for their size, the mites run as fast as a cheetah, an attribute which equips them for the task of racing from lengthy flower to bill and into the nasal passages (or vice versa) in preparation for their voyage. They have only a brief instant to make the dash while the hummingbird hovers at the blossom. Colwell estimates that there are some 500 species of hummingbird flower mite. Many of them show considerable specificity for certain species of flower, including heliconias. Males may be armed with massive spines or raptorial legs that they use to crunch their rivals. If you dissect a blossom and use a magnifying glass to scan its interior, you may find these mites — tiny, pale and obscure but tough and determined.

On a heliconia in Peru, I found what must be one of the richest assemblages of treehoppers, relatives of aphids. Treehoppers are attractive, if diminutive, sap-sucking insects, noted for their weird appearance. Part of their exoskeleton, the pronotum, covers most of their body and is often sculpted into inexplicable shapes — balls and spikes, with pockmarked and pitted textures, striped, blotched and polka-dotted in colour schemes that range from the most cryptic simulations of caterpillar frass to bold blacks and oranges. Like many aphids, these insects often associate with ants and exchange services with them. The sap-suckers excrete sugar-rich fluids that the ants collect and eat, and the ants chase away such potential predators of membracid nymphs and eggs as ladybird beetles

bats will cluster u
The reasons for tl
remain a mystery
special effort to c
they move on to

New heliconia
tunnel that is use
nal animals. Disk
onto the slick leaf
like structures on
earwigs are even
frog is tucked insi
cone. I once four
katydid, a preda
During its noctur
out; when a passi
did lurches forwa
its sharp, powerf
did out of the lea
ger hard enough
other mark of goc
to get close enou
them to bite you

The heliconia p
range of insects t
largest butterflie
huge owl-eyed C;

The vine snake (*Oxybelis brevirostris*) intricately coiled about the vibrant inflorescence of *Heliconia trichocarpa* is able to prey upon lizards that seek out heliconia plants to sun themselves or to hunt their own prey.

81

Several species of
cluding these *Ec*
use heliconias a:
day. The bats cl
veins on either s
midrib, causing
down, thus crea
from the sun an
ing their exposu

The sophistication of this
katydid's (*Mimetica incisa*) camouflage is best appreciated when
the insect is considered in its natural environment. The mix of
light and shadow and the great
variety of leaf shades and hues
provide a complex background
that is confusing to visual
predators.

Highly venomous, bushmasters (*Lachesis muta*), above, may reach lengths of more than 2.5 metres. The mottled pattern that blends with the leaf litter serves primarily to allow it to hunt mammals as a sit-and-wait predator. Right: In the event of an attack by a bird, a false eye spot located on the edge of the hind wing of the glasswing butterfly (*Cithaerias* spp) deflects the peck away from vital body parts.

ness. The mottled young tapir or fawn may be innocuous and prime fare for many predators, but other cryptically patterned animals — jaguars and anacondas, for example — are not; the purpose of their camouflage is for concealment when hunting.

It is these large camouflaged predators which provide the most psychologically impressive demonstrations of the effectiveness of disruptive colorations. On one of my field trips in Costa Rica, I warned the students about the danger of overlooking such animals when walking along the trails. They did not really believe my warnings; in fact, I did not take them seriously enough myself.

On our first hike, there were plenty of conspicuous distractions — a blue-flowering *Faramea* shrub and some spectacular fig-tree crowns adorned with newly flushed leaves. We sauntered along the trail casually, eyes up, when suddenly, the student behind me let loose a gasp and a garbled but unmistakable exclamation of alarm. I stopped dead and looked in the direction of his gesticulating hand. Finally, it dawned upon me that I was a mere metre away from a very large fer-de-lance coiled neatly beside the path.

We backed up and waited for the other students bringing up the rear, who experienced the same problem I had: they had to walk to within two metres of it and have it pointed out before they could really see it. That is an unsettling feature of both the fer-de-lance and the much larger and more formidable bushmaster. Both snakes are cryptically patterned, with glossy skin crosshatched in browns, greys and tans that render them difficult to detect even at short range. We learned later that half a dozen students ahead of us had passed right by the snake, blissfully oblivious to its presence.

Most of us would be happier if the fer-de-lance had evolved a luminescent lemon skin marked with purple stripes. Such warning coloration would save the snake unwanted encounters that can lead to the waste of its venom and to broken fangs, and it would prevent numerous deaths and mutilations of the many *campesinos* who step on or pass too close to this relatively pugnacious viper. Instead, the pattern of a fer-de-lance is the evolutionary triumph of crypsis over advertisement. Along with bushmasters, boas, pythons, anacondas and many rattlers, the fer-de-lance has a camouflage pattern. These big reptiles are all ambush-style predators: they sit and wait for their prey to blunder within striking range. Food is far more important to them than warning away potential predators and wandering heavy-footed mammals.

There is a kind of horror that comes with this discovery about the big snakes, but few naturalists will forgo a chance to see one of the legendary serpents in the field. Typically, someone tells you there is a fer-de-lance or bushmaster right over there at the base of the tree. You go over carefully, excited about getting your first look at one of the most dangerous snakes in the Americas. You inch ahead, aware that a fer-de-lance is willing to strike when threatened and that the two-centimetre fangs can deliver a voluminous gush of tissue-destroying toxins. Your eyes search the leaf litter closely but see no snake. You lean closer, head extended and everything else held back; you stare yet see nothing. You advance a little more, and still more, until suddenly and awfully, it materializes, a huge puddle of snake coiled right before your eyes.

By then, you are close enough to see all the details that formerly were just part of the blur of light and shade, old leaves and twigs. Up close, you see the lustre of the skin that gives it its Costa Rican name "velvet." You see the hard, impersonal yellow eyes, the malevolent eyebrow ridges and the huge wedge-shaped head swelling at the base. Can those be the venom glands? The large pits in the nasal area of the face, its infrared heat-sensing organs, are remarkably deep. You wonder how you missed it before, yet when you stand back, the monster virtually dissolves into the forest floor. With a sinking feeling, you realize just how many more you have missed in the past and how many you will miss again.

At such moments, the words of British zoologist Hugh Cott, preeminent student of adaptive coloration, come to mind. When we are lucky enough to see the hidden and their artistry is revealed, especially in this form, we had best "look on in wonder and in gratitude."

Three-toed sloths (*Bradypus infuscatus*) are often observed in *Cecropia* trees, whose leaves are a preferred food. The open, sunny architecture of this tree makes it relatively easy to see the cryptic mammal.

Buffon, who never saw a sloth in its arboreal haunts, may have been puzzled by the difficulty sloths have in getting around a conventional animal cage or human domicile. An old natural-history book I have, a work compiled in 1823, contains an illustration of a sloth that was no doubt drawn by some British artist working from a stuffed museum specimen. It shows the sloth standing erect in a curious quadruped posture, with its long forelegs and shorter hind legs forcing it into a sprinter's stance. Its long claws curve along the ground. However, as naturalist Charles Waterton pointed out, such a posture would have been unachievable, for "the sloth has no heels." In reality, a sloth on the ground is a gruesomely awkward sight. Because it is literally incapable of standing upright, its belly scrapes against the earth. Its limbs sprawl and splay fore and aft, and it can move only by reaching ahead, wrapping its claws around some fixed object or digging them into the soil and dragging its body across the ground. In this position, the sloth is not only ludicrous but — more important — defenceless. One can imagine why Buffon, who observed the sloth in this state, summed it up as "the picture of innate misery."

A sloth must hang; it is at its best when suspended upside down from a horizontal limb. In that position, it can do all it needs to do — feed, sleep, breed, walk and whistle. Waterton, who travelled in the Guianas, was one of the first naturalists to see sloths in the field. He countered

Buffon's assessment by pointing out that "this singular animal is destined by nature to live and die in the trees; and to do justice to him, naturalists must examine him in his upper element." That perspective should be brought to our consideration of all organisms: we are blind to the virtues and splendour of an organism if we do not see it in the place where it evolved.

The sloth's most conspicuous adaptation to the upper echelons of rainforest is its feet. Essentially large hooks, they have been reduced in complexity and width, drawn out and tipped with long claws able to curve around small limbs. The last joints of the digits do the holding. A much more effective way to grasp a tubular surface than with a fist, the sloth's hooklike grip remains strong even when the wrist is being twisted and rotated. The sloth's limb joints are very loosely encapsulated, and the articulating bones have rounded surfaces without the channels and flanges that constrain and strengthen most joints, allowing for acrobatic manoeuvring. In fact, the sloth's feet can rotate almost 180 degrees. Try this with your own feet; even ballet dancers can manage only 90 degrees. The sloth is thus able to move with slow but superb agility along the branching array of lianas and tree limbs that constitute its highways.

The consequence of the sloth's special foot structure is a dependence on thin supports; it cannot manage well on a hefty horizontal branch. Apparently limited to localities with plenty of lianas, sloths are, however, good swimmers and make reasonable headway with a long-limbed dog paddle. (This serves them in good stead in riverbank and floodplain habitats, which, although often liana-poor, support relatively nutritious types of vegetation, including *Cecropia* trees. Even the sloth sometimes falls off a limb into the water.)

The oldest natural-history book in my collection was written by someone ignorant of the fact that sloths are able to move smoothly through the canopy on their network of lianas and limbs. The author concocted the following rather ingenious theory of movement: "The sloth subsists entirely on vegetable food, and as it requires a considerable share of provision, it generally strips a tree of all its verdure in less than a fortnight. It then falls to devouring the bark and thus in a short time destroys the very source of its support. When this is the case, being unable to descend, it is obliged to drop from the branches to the ground; and after remaining some time torpid, from the violence of its fall, it prepares for a tedious, dangerous and painful migration to some neighbouring tree."

That creative scenario may have been stimulated by the fact that sloths do seem to be almost moribund at times. Even when fully awake, they move so slowly that it can be almost painful to watch. This apparent laziness gives the sloth its popular name in both Spanish and English

(the lazy) and is explained by the Bororo tribes with the following myth:

"Long ago, the sloth was not easygoing. He moved rapidly through the forest and had a nasty, greedy temperament. One day, the Almighty decided to descend to Earth. He waited four weeks until the hole in the sky known as the moon was fully open, and then He climbed down on a liana. On His arrival, He went to drink at a water hole. A group of animals—a tapir, a hare, a jaguar, an anteater and others—all stepped aside so that He could drink first. All but the sloth. The sloth pushed ahead and drank greedily and at great length. This, of course, angered the Almighty One, and He announced to the sloth that in punishment, He would cast a spell. The terrified sloth expected death. But the Almighty just breathed on him, snuffing out forever his greed and thirst. With great relief, the sloth smiled, and since then, he has never had another drink and has been as easygoing as they get."

If we doubt this account, we need not accept instead Buffon's claim that the sloth's idleness is a consequence of wretched design. It is more accurately described as superb energy conservation. The sloth's metabolism is as specialized as its morphology and reflects the requirements of life as an arboreal leaf eater.

The three-toed sloth's low-energy diet is made up of large volumes of leaves whose many calories are bound up in hard-to-digest cellulose. A huge, multichambered stomach that functions much like the digestive system of cows and other ruminants fills one-third of the sloth's body and is rich in bacteria capable of digesting cellulose. The leaves may spend as long as a month in the stomach before moving on to the small intestine. But a high-fibre diet digested on this small scale apparently does not produce the calories necessary to sustain the elevated body temperatures typical of mammals. Instead, the sloth's body temperature fluctuates, rising in daytime as it forages and declining at night or when it is sleeping and digestion is taking place.

At the best of times, however, the sloth's body temperature is low, ranging from 30 to 34 degrees C—well below the 37 degrees typical of humans and the even higher temperatures of smaller mammals. At night, it may drop close to ambient temperatures in the 20s. Body size seems to affect the distribution and activity patterns of the two major types of sloths. The larger two-toed sloths occupy tropical mountain slopes and range into the cloud forest, while the three-toed sloths remain confined to lower elevations. Perhaps because of their greater energy requirements, the three-toed sloths are more active both day and night than are their two-toed relatives.

When at rest, a sloth does its best to pull itself into a compact, hanging-basket shape by moving its long, heat-radiating feet toward each other on the limb. In a tree crotch, it assumes a completely spherical posture, bury-

Sloths travel through the canopy along a network of horizontal branches and vines, moving limb over limb, suspended by their hooklike claws. On the ground, sloths are less agile, dragging themselves along rather than standing erect like most quadrupeds.

121

ing its nearly naked clown face in its chest fur. Its long, shaggy fur coat looks more appropriate for an Arctic mammal than for a denizen of the sweltering, humid Tropics, but in fact, the hairiness of the sloth is in part an adaptation to conserve heat. Special grooves on each hair support blue-green algae that undergo population explosions according to the regime of rainfall. During the dry season, sloths turn grey and brown, growing darker and greener when the rains come. This mossy, coarse pelage gives them a cryptic, poorly defined shape when they hang immobile overhead. The Machiguenga Indians of the eastern Peruvian lowlands, who, like all tribes, have their own names for the constellations of stars, thus apply their word for sloth to the amorphous twin galaxies, the Magellanic Clouds. (The Brazilian Mundurucú have seized on a shorter-range image of the sloth. When seen from a few metres away, a sloth looks much like a hanging weaving. The Mundurucú therefore credit the sloth with the invention of the hammock, which veterans of languid tropical afternoons acknowledge as one of the finest discoveries known to civilization.)

All of these features allow the well-insulated, slow-burning sloth to make do with only half the normal metabolic rate of other comparably sized mammals. But there is a cost to such thermal conservation: the need to reactivate on cool mornings. A sloth does not have a large muscle mass capable of generating much heat through shivering, nor does it have the mass to retain heat once it is generated. Instead, it raises its temperature by sunbathing. At dawn, the sloth will dangle from the peak of the eastern face of a tree crown, basking more like some strangely hairy, tailless reptile than a warm-blooded mammal. Sunbathing literally warms its blood.

This is also the time that the three-toed sloth exposes a brilliant orange-red patch of fine fur along its back. This single flamboyant act has earned it the aboriginal name "sun sloth" in some areas, and while the skin flag's social significance is unknown, either mate attraction or territorial advertisement are possibilities. Although the three-toed sloth will now and then whistle in monotones, other aspects of its social life seem remarkably dull; copulation appears to be a rare event. And there is only one report, an eyewitness account by herpetologist Harry Greene, of two sloths fighting, apparently for possession of a *Cecropia* tree.

The sloth's seemingly minimal use of visual signals may account for its strikingly rigid facial expressions. In keeping with the economy of the sloth, which has one of the lowest muscle weights of all mammals relative to its size and limb lengths, its facial musculature is greatly reduced except for the chewing apparatus. The fixed, almost smiling expression is particularly noticeable in the three-toed sloth and is perhaps coupled with the low intelligence quotient that most folivores appear to possess.

A recent natural-history text notes that the sloth's "sadly vacuous expression gives the impression that it entertains an actual thought on alternate Tuesdays."

There may be a good ecological reason for such undemonstrative behaviour. Social signals such as whistling or exposing its orange back flag—even sunbathing or just plain movement—make the sloth vulnerable to predation because of its slow speed. Although human hunters complain that sloths seem to be composed mainly of hair, bone and stringy sinews, many animals, given the opportunity, will eat sloths; friends of mine have seen them killed by tayra weasels and pumas.

Sloths are not completely defenceless. Their limbs

time spans days ;
for howlers and

Contrary to tl
howlers have a
they are not ave
terlopers with th
They are often (
nation of height
pact that canno
penter saw the h
as a sign of inte
would slowly ap
as nearly as pc
ment . . . . Seen
crement is a kinc
words, the act o
tool use. In any
differences betw
sloth and the hc

Howlers let go
waking at dawn.
noise and the voo
of daytime clock
structed in Euro
songs. What this
is that howlers e
create new spac
sloths and howl
gent procedure t
nivore. Both hav
sis; otherwise, t

The scatologi
sloths goes furtl
gous (dung-eatii
ulation in Brazil
species of copro
with its dung—n
Howler dung ha
followers and fe
than two dozen s

have a slow but amazing strength, not unlike that of a pneumatic piston moving inexorably in its designated direction. If a sloth wants to drag its great hooked nails across your body, you had better move out of the way. The two-toed sloth is especially pugnacious compared with the three-toed, and it will advertise the menace of its claws by hanging by its hind feet with its forelimbs spread, showing its prominent hooked toes, mouth agape and expelling air. It is a ritualized display with a convincing message. It is also a good chance to see how incredibly stained the sloth's large side teeth are by its diet of tannin- and alkaloid-laced leaves; the teeth are the same hue as those of one of my tobacco-chewing neighbours.

After it is detected, the sloth's best defence is distance. A sloth, whether threatened or resting, can usually dangle from thin lianas that are inaccessible to most arboreal cats and weasels. But the keen-eyed harpy eagle, the world's heaviest eagle, with wrists as thick as your own and talons as long as a grizzly's claws, is able to snag the sloth, yank it from its holdfast and use the lifting power of its huge, broad wings to carry it off. Several different (and highly courageous) studies of harpy nests have found that the sloth constitutes the single largest component of the harpy's diet, followed by monkeys, porcupines, opossums and other mammals.

The presence of a harpy or other predator must have a considerable impact on sloth populations. I suspect such predation was common until the recent extirpation of large predators in areas such as Barro Colorado Island and much of Costa Rica. That may be one reason sloths show little evidence of territoriality. Considerable overlap in the home range of sloths occurs without any overt hostility when they are close together. Along a river canal in northeastern Costa Rica, I saw three adult three-toed sloths all within sight of each other. Natural predation rates in areas that still retain harpy eagles, cats and other predators, coupled with the sloth's slow metabolism, may keep populations below the carrying capacity of the vegetation. In addition, the reproductive rate of sloths is low; after the two-toed sloth's 304-day pregnancy, a single offspring is born, and there is a long interval between successive births.

A lean diet combined with arboreality probably explains the low birth weight of sloths. One of the rare measurements of a newborn three-toed sloth revealed that its weight was only 5 percent that of an adult. That is a low figure as many mammals go (considering that only a single offspring is born) and one that is on a par with human birth weights. And also like humans, the sloth offspring are slow to mature. The infant three-toed sloth clings to its mother for a full six months before becoming independent.

Like all adaptations, those of the sloth cannot be fully appreciated in taxonomic isolation any more than they

Although they are slow-moving, three-toed sloths (*Bradypus infuscatus*) are highly acrobatic. They climb, dangle and manoeuvre with the great agility afforded by their flexible joints and long, powerful limbs, left. The female two-toed sloth (*Choloepus hoffmanni*), above, carries her single offspring with her for several months until the young sloth can forage on its own.

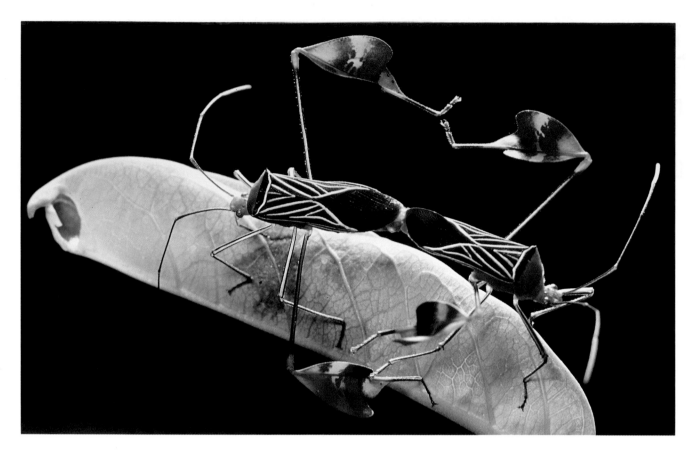

were hideous and painful but preferable to the effects of grenades, heavy artillery and mustard gas.

My account of this biochemical horror story is not meant to repel anyone considering a foray into tropical forest; there are plenty of temperate-zone insects that also produce toxic substances. My point is simply an ecological one: it appears to me that the proportion of rainforest insects with chemical defences is relatively high. There are several reasons why we might expect this to be the case. Some ecologists believe that the ratio of predators to prey and the ecological importance of predation as opposed to other causes of mortality —the weather, for example —are highest in rainforest.

The mating pair of flag-footed bugs (*Anisocelis flavolineata*), above, produces noxious, malodorous secretions when disturbed, but their specialized, colourful hind legs make it easy for predators such as birds to learn to avoid them. The bold pattern of the freshly emerged passion-vine butterfly (*Heliconius hewitsoni*), right, is a form of warning coloration that advertises unpalatability.

up, perhaps oxidized and attacked by Dave's own defensive enzymes. Then the wound began to heal just like a regular, heat-induced burn.

This toxic rove beetle is a member of the genus *Paederus,* comprising some 600 species found around the world but especially prevalent in wet, tropical habitats. *Paederus*'s greatest threat to humans is that its deadly secretion can cause blindness, a common event in areas where mass emergences take place. (The investigators who first purified pederin were able to collect 100 million beetles, the quantity needed to extract enough toxin to perform the chemical analysis, from just one such mass emergence.) Pederin, incidentally, is not all bad as far as humans are concerned. Like many toxins, it has medical value when judiciously applied in tiny amounts. A Chinese manuscript written in the year 739 suggests that it could be used to remove tattoos and to treat boils and ringworm. Further benefits have been confirmed by more recent studies. The application of small amounts to areas of skin with dermatosis, such as eczema and chronic sores and ulcers, especially in older patients, effected complete healing where all other treatments had failed. Perhaps the most original use of this beetle was made by eastern-European males who had the intelligence to see that serving in World War I was not adaptive behaviour. Collecting two species of *Paederus*, they obtained medical exemptions by using pederin to induce ulcers and inflammations that

As a result, rainforest organisms such as insects would invest relatively greater amounts of their resources in developing and maintaining antipredator chemistry.

A related factor is that many rainforest insects are long-lived. Tropical butterflies such as *Heliconius* are known to survive the better part of a year. Such long exposure to predators increases the value of a chemical defence system. By comparison, short-lived insects that have a brief adult stage, like mayflies and midges, lack any chemical defences.

The true extent of invertebrate defences is just being unearthed. Only 900 beetle species have been chemically surveyed —a tiny fraction of the millions that exist. Yet that small sample has revealed an astonishing repertoire of secretions, a collection of chemical structures with intriguing biological properties. Some beetles produce antifungal and antibacterial compounds such as methyl-8-hydroxyquinoline-2-carboxylate, a dual-purpose secretion that also acts as a predator deterrent by causing intestinal spasms in mice. Other secretions such as colymbetin lower the blood pressure of mammals. Bombardier beetles mix quinones and peroxides together and jet out a burning spray that they can direct with great accuracy. The two chemicals are mixed at the point of discharge, producing an explosive heat-generating reaction that sprays out a caustic mixture with a temperature of 100 degrees C, as hot as boiling water.

Various other beetle secretions rival pederin for potency. Bushmen in the Kalahari use the oral secretion of *Diamphidia simplex* to make poison arrows; the ooze from a single insect can destroy a large mammal. The cantharidin of "Spanish fly" fame is a secretion common in meloid blister beetles and is so highly toxic that the Merck manual says it causes "severe gastroenteritis, melena, renal damage, haematuria, spermatorrhea, priapism, profound collapse and death." One wonders what gruesome circumstances yielded this information. At least some of the symptoms were described from a particular case of poisoning. French soldiers stationed in Algiers ate a meal of frogs that had themselves dined on a large number of meloid beetles. The cantharidin had thus made its way up the food chain, and as it passed through the soldiers' digestive systems and urinary tracts, it caused severe disturbances, including "*érections douloureuses et prolongées.*" Vertebrate predators, however, are almost certainly not the principal selective force responsible for the evolution of cantharidin.

Male meloids alone synthesize cantharidin, using it as a nuptial gift to females. The compound is transferred to the female during mating. She then coats her eggs with cantharidin as they are laid so that it functions as an egg protector. Ants are known to be repelled by minute traces of the secretion, and since ants groom leaf surfaces and remove insect eggs, such a transfer benefits both partners quite apart from enhancing their survival.

Few tropical vertebrates possess any significant chemical weaponry. Mammals produce plenty of interesting and complex excretions, but the vast majority are social signals for mate attraction and territorial marking. Skunks are the only mammals with a defence comparable to that of a bombardier beetle. Birds have scarcely any defensive excretions, with the exception of vultures and various seabirds that regurgitate bilious fluids on intruders. Likewise, lizards, turtles and snakes have few overt chemical defences. Some snakes and turtles have sour-smelling cloacal discharges, but they lack the irritant authority of many invertebrate-generated molecules. Snake venoms can be a formidable deterrent, but they are first and foremost feeding adaptations. Only the spitting cobras of Africa and Southeast Asia use venoms for deterrence at a distance.

Most of the chemical defences found in rainforest, then, belong to plants and arthropods. They pose a threat only to those intent on browsing at random or to entomologists conditioned by their strange subculture to grab at almost any new specimen without restraint. The average visitor has little to fear from rainforest plants and insects. From time to time, however, almost every tropical naturalist has a purely accidental brush with a well-defended insect.

The last experience I had akin to Dave's burning bee-

tles was also caused by the slightest contact with an insect in Monteverde. I was walking along an overgrown trail through thick second growth on a west-facing slope. The late-afternoon sun was hot, and I had made the mistake of thoughtlessly rolling up my shirtsleeves. An electrifying prickling on my bare forearm startled me. I looked at my arm but saw nothing. Then a series of red welts began to materialize on the white skin, giving a colourful calligraphic form to the rising wave of torment. I knew what the agency was; the question was, Where were they? One hates to suffer pain and not see the source. I looked behind me at the vegetation. A metre back, I found them on a small shrub: a cluster of very large and decorative silk-moth caterpillars. The size of small cigars, they were green with red flecks and long, elegantly branched and star-tufted spines. It was the delicate tracery of those spines that traumatized my skin and left it itching for days after the pain subsided. Caterpillars with irritating hairs are known the world over, but temperate forms usually have only mildly toxic properties. Some tropical families, notably the Megalopigidae, take the stinging defence a step further, having evolved specialized spines that act as hypodermic injectors of potent venom. These beautiful caterpillars look like the antithesis of nastiness.

A bull's-eye silk moth (*Automeris rubrescens*) displays the brightly coloured eye spots on its hind wings. The sudden appearance of a pair of staring eyes is intended to "startle" small vertebrate predators into fleeing. But the display is pure bluff: the moth's bright colours are not associated with a noxious taste.

One common Peruvian species of megalopigid caterpillar is known as the *cuy dorado*, or golden guinea pig. It looks like a tiny furry mammal with a soft, longhaired yet neatly combed coat. But to touch one can be among the world's worst experiences. Underneath the soft hairs are sharp, venom-injecting spines. In addition to histamine, the venom contains proteins that destroy blood cells and tissue. Doctors excel at describing the horrible impact of these compounds, which "begins with stinging, immediately followed by an intense burning pain; a few minutes later, a diffuse area of erythema develops. This area, within 2 to 15 minutes, will show whitish edematous hemispheric papules, about two to three millimetres in diameter . . . . They may coalesce and form an urticarial weal, with a whitish rough surface, which itches violently for one hour or more. Within 24 hours, the lesion will have developed into a congestive and slightly edematous cord showing numerous isolated or coalescent vesicles and sometimes blisters. These later break up, spontaneously or by trauma, and develop into erosions or excoriations that dry up and, five to seven days after the

sting, become covered with scabby small crusts." Of course, poison ivy can produce the same sort of horror on one's hide, but victims of these delicate caterpillars vomit and pass out from the pain. Remarkably, that did not prevent various Brazilian tribes from using them to inflame and swell their genitals for recreational purposes.

The bright colours and bold patterns of these insects are no coincidence. Most well-defended insects advertise their unpalatability with a strong form of sign language that discourages birds and other visual predators from pecking at them. One can use this pattern to make some crude judgments about the wisdom of handling an unknown insect. However, even if one avoids touching insects, one can still get burned. A few insect weapons are released even as one approaches and peers at the insect. There are reduviid assassin bugs from Zanzibar which reportedly spray a saliva that is pharmacologically similar to cobra venom. The saliva contains proteins that break down tissue, cause paralysis and contain hyaluronidase, the enzyme common to snake venoms and leech saliva, the "spreading factor" which breaks down tissue and allows the venom to disperse rapidly. Spraying their digestive juices perhaps enables these assassin bugs to deter birds or monkeys that would suffer from an eyeful.

Because of the surprising range of arthropod sprays, one occasionally gets coated with one of them quite unexpectedly. Both millipedes and stink bugs can spray their mixtures of benzaldehyde and hydrogen cyanide for distances of up to half a metre. For those who enjoy amaretto or almond cookies, the scent of the combination can have delicious and pleasant connotations. But when the substance is applied, it can be horrible. While trying to navigate through a thicket in southern Borneo, I stuck my head down in order to plough through a small archway of vines. As I passed under the vegetation, I got a full dose of the acrid spray of a stink bug, a burning, eye-watering mixture that had an oil-of-almond aroma. Often such secretions contain hydrocarbons and solvents that are designed to allow the caustic toxic compounds to penetrate the skin rapidly. It felt as though my face were being oxidized, and no doubt there would have been skin damage if I had not washed it off.

The mechanism millipedes employ for producing cyanide gas has been elegantly worked out by Tom Eisner, an ecologist who specializes in arthropod defences. Free-cyanide compounds would poison the millipedes themselves if they were stored in active form. Instead, the millipedes—in this case, polydesmids, a group common in the rainforest understorey—mix them as needed. The millipede has a series of chambers distributed along its body segments. Each chamber is full of an inert fluid made up of a compound called mandelonitrile. The chamber can be emptied with a muscular squeeze that forces the liquid to the outside by passing it through a smaller

chamber. This chamber contains an enzyme that breaks down the mandelonitrile into hydrogen-cyanide gas and benzaldehyde. As the reacting mixture emerges from the body, it produces a protective cloud of toxic gas that surrounds the quiescent millipede for 30 minutes or more.

Many plants produce similar cyanide-generating compounds. Wild sapotes (*Pouteria* spp), for example, impregnate their green fruits with the cyanide-based prussic acid. If you find one of these avocado-sized fruits while it is still green and slice it open with a pocketknife, white fluid oozes from the flesh and the smell of almonds fills the air. The presence of the compound no doubt helps defend the immature seed from attacks by agoutis and other seed-eating rodents. Comparable products are apparently released from the roots of various *Prunus* species (a group with both tropical and temperate members such as peaches and cherries) as an aggressive territorial defence against other plant competitors.

It makes a lot of sense for toxin-generating insects to expel their defensive chemicals in advance of an attack, thus minimizing the risk that a naïve predator will damage the insect with an exploratory peck or a trial tasting. It is not always successful. Eisner reports on a laboratory interaction between a walking stick with a toxic spray and a *Marmosa* mouse opossum, an important insect predator found in Central and South American rainforest. Eisner watched the marmosa attack the walking

stick and promptly receive a spray on its muzzle. The irritation was obvious — the marmosa dashed about wiping its face, but all the while, it held on to the walking stick with its paw. Eventually, the spray was exhausted and the marmosa was able to eat the walking stick. Little larger than a shrew, the marmosa has the ferocious appetite required to fuel a small, heat-radiating body, and it will risk noxious irritation to avoid starvation. Eisner also reports that the tiny and voracious grasshopper mouse, another insect specialist with representatives in tropical Central American rainforest, will attack and eat beetles that have toxic sprays.

Perhaps such chemical emissions will not serve for desperate specialists such as mouse opossums, but I know from experience that they work well on larger vertebrates. Not only do some of them irritate the skin, mucous membranes and eyes, but they also taste terrible. I have been surprised on several occasions by the chemical defences of danaid butterflies and pericopid moths. The former are often patterned in oranges and blacks, and the latter are beautiful creatures sporting bold patterns of luminous blues and heavy reds set on a deep navy-blue background. When they are molested, a bubbly froth flows out of the pores in the upper thorax. Once I touched a minuscule dab of this foam to the tip of my tongue and was rewarded with an enduring vile bitterness that lasted for several hours and resisted my efforts to wash it away.

The larva of the bull's-eye silk moth (*Automeris rubrescens*) is far better protected than the adult moth. Its delicate spines are a bristly, stinging defence. With even the slightest contact, the spines break off in the skin, and the toxic chemicals they contain cause immediate and excruciating pain.

131

No chemical defence is completely effective against all predators. This green lynx spider, a member of the Oxyopidae family, has managed to overcome a young stink bug. Invertebrates such as spiders are often not affected by defensive chemicals that serve to deter vertebrate predators.

Perhaps the ultimate in chemical repellency over a long distance is a tropical hornet's nest. One is often advised, "If you don't bother them, they won't bother you." Unfortunately, that is not universally true. Many of the 700 species of tropical social wasp are docile and attack only when the colony is being ravaged. However, a few species with large colonies and thousands of resident workers have a great deal to lose and can afford to expend a few workers in defence of the colony. Such species will mount an attack even if one stands innocently some distance from the hive. I have been chased off by *Polybia* and assorted *Stelopolybia* wasps when I have been as far as five metres from the nest. The wasps appear acutely sensitive to the odour of mammalian sweat, and the slightest vibration of their nesting tree sends them swarming. They fly at your head and eyes and, at the moment of impact, turn their abdomen down toward your skin, the better to drive home their barbed stingers. Like honeybee workers, the whole apparatus is designed to leave the stinger securely embedded, with its sac of venom feeding poison into your body. As with most insects, it is not the physical impact but chemistry, a soup of tissue-cleaving enzymes and histamine, that does the discouraging.

The coordinated social order and communication systems of these societies are designed to target and apply the venomous defence before the nest can be physically damaged. Often, the sentinel worker wasps on the nest comb will drum their abdomens vigorously on the nest surface, summoning up a frenzy of additional defenders from within. Some of the aerial attackers actually spray venom into the air around you, a release that acts as an alarm signal, identifying the threat and inciting more stinging.

But a specialist predator can circumvent even this group defence. Capuchin monkeys such as *Cebus apella* get almost half their food from hornet nests. Ecologist John Terborgh, who has conducted the longest-running project on Neotropical monkey foraging, told me this long ago. But having studied the wasps for several years and having experienced their considerable weaponry, I found it difficult to believe any primate would risk such injury for a fistful of grubs. (My own excuse was that I was after a Ph.D.) When I visited Terborgh's study site in Peru's Manú Park, however, I saw an astounding case of monkey versus hornet that made me a believer.

I was doing my laundry in the clearing, a grassy yard with a few shrubs surrounded by a wall of forest. A large male capuchin monkey was sitting in a tree, peering down into the clearing. Monkeys pass through the area with great frequency, so I paid it little mind. It moved closer to the clothesline, paused and leapt out into the clearing, grabbing onto the trunk of a dead *Cecropia* tree. It won a little more of my attention when it began to descend, something monkeys are loath to do in the presence of

humans. Once on the ground, it took two quick hops to a shrub and bounded into the air, reaching up with both arms. It came down with a hornet's nest the size of a soccer ball in its hands. A cloud of disoriented wasps poured out as it sprang across the clearing shaking its prize. In a few seconds, it was working its way through the treetops again.

The monkey had relied on suddenness for its success. No doubt, it received a few stings, but most of the wasps remained swarming confusedly around the shrub. As its reward, the capuchin had many combs packed with tender white larvae. While to me the heist appeared premeditated, practised, intelligent and even courageous, the behavioural and ecological significance of the monkey's action was its effectiveness in circumventing the wasps' ability to mount a coordinated defence. Perhaps that is why these hornets often attack first when given the chance. They cannot respond to an unanticipated all-out assault and social disruption. Against such an intelligent predator, the best defence is a discouraging preemptive strike. If you are stung for no apparent reason, you may credit it to that.

Temperate-tropical differences in host-plant defences may also contribute to the trend toward tropical toxicity. Many herbivorous insects extract poisons from their host plants. Often, insect defensive compounds are nitrogen-rich alkaloids of complex construction. It is well known that the proportion of plants containing alkaloids increases as one moves from the high latitudes toward the equator; proportionately twice as many tropical plants contain alkaloids as do nontropical plants. Why this should be is a matter of guesswork, but perhaps the unrelenting presence and pressure of leaf-eating insects has an impact in the Tropics. In the land where winter never comes, there is probably less weather-induced insect mortality than in higher latitudes. In response, tropical plants must invest relatively more in anti-insect defences.

Insects that specialize in certain plants can develop immunity to defensive compounds and turn them to their own ends, which means that the opportunities for herbivorous insects to sequester defensive alkaloids from plants are greatest in the Tropics. Sometimes, as in the case of *Paederus*, the insect synthesizes its own toxins. This is especially true for the many arthropods, including carpenter ants, various caterpillars and vinegarroons, that use simple compounds such as formic and acetic acid (vinegar). Often, herbivorous insects use their host plants as a source of chemical weaponry.

The squash and cucumber family, a primarily tropical one of about 800 species of sprawling and climbing vines, affords a classic example. One can often find a vine of some sort in tropical-forestlike gaps that clearly resembles a small cucumber or squash. Do not taste the fruit; most are laced with various oxygenated tetracyclic triter-

The red and black colour of these mating giant millipedes is associated with their ability to produce cyanide-rich defensive secretions.

penes, more commonly known as cucurbitacins. Our domesticated cucumber is edible only because one of our ancestors living in the forests of India discovered and husbanded fruits with few of these defensive compounds. Cucurbitacin is the most bitter substance known. It is detectable by humans at concentrations as low as one part per billion. Accidentally tasting a well-defended wild cucumber fruit can cause a person to collapse with nausea and to suffer severe cramps and diarrhea for days. A minuscule dose, a millionth of a mammal's body weight, can be fatal.

The evolutionary integration of cucurbitacins by some ancestral cucumber was no doubt one of the keys to the success of this plant family. One might expect such an adaptation to allow an ancestral species to become widespread and subsequently speciated during the epoch in which the plants were relatively immune to herbivory. But all good defences are eventually breached. Certain beetles have accomplished the feat and are now positively attracted to the taste and odour of these compounds. Cucumber beetles outdo even our response to these molecules, exceeding the sensitivity of the most sophisticated chemical-survey techniques. Not only are these elegant black-and-yellow-striped beetles immune to the toxic properties of cucurbitacins, but they actually load up on them. That is why cucumber beetles can become agricultural pests; their ability to consume plant toxins prevents most predators from attacking them. And as specialists on cucurbits, they have relatively little competition from more generalized herbivores.

Plants also produce defensive hormones, but most appear to be directed against the physiology of insects. Many ferns and conifers create compounds that are closely related to the growth and moulting hormones of insects, in effect causing a hormonal imbalance that makes it impossible for the insects to grow. If this sounds rather sophisticated for a plant, that is because it is. Plants can neither run nor hide from their predators, and in response to grazing pressure, they have evolved a remarkable array of chemical defences. In addition to being hydrogen-cyanide generators and hormone mimics, plants are also impregnated with tannin and phenols which inhibit digestion, vast numbers of poisonous alkaloids, relatives of mustard gas, opiates, saponin, hallucinogens, vitamin- and protein-destroying enzymes and essential oils that destroy beneficial gut bacteria. Plants contain as much molecular weaponry as insects do, yet we pass by them in the forest, unaware of the toxic presence hidden in greenery.

There are, however, significant exceptions. Tropical nettles can be unforgiving of even the slightest contact. In a remarkable convergence with stinging caterpillars, nettle hairs are laced with histamine, which causes a massive allergic reaction, and with acetylcholine, which is in-

The ithomiine butterfly (*Thyridia psidii*) that emerges from the pupa, seen suspended here among begonia seeds, may already possess defensive chemicals that are derived from the plants upon which the larvae feed.

volved in carrying impulses through the nervous system. Presumably, the latter aids in firing the skin's network of pain receptors. I have been stung by both northern nettles and tropical nettles. There is no doubt that the latter group, which includes some species with conspicuous red spines, is better at inducing loud cursing and dancing in the careless.

Often, the toxicity of a plant is correlated with the appearance and toxicity of the insects that feed on it. Many tropical plants in the milkweed, Apocynaceae, Euphorbiaceae and Moraceae families are protected by a white, chemically toxic sap, and these plants often cater to insect herbivores that are warningly coloured and presumably chemically defended. A common hazard in New World rainforest is a tree known appropriately as *Sapium*. It is found in second growth and forest edges of montane rainforest, the sort of spot where one flails indiscriminately with a machete to clear passage. When *Sapium* is cut, it immediately exudes large amounts of white sap capable of causing blindness if even a single droplet lands in an eye.

Insects that feed on the white-sapped plants are often brilliantly marked with warning colours. The large and conspicuous sphinx moth feeds on frangipani (*Plumeria rubra*). This bold black-and-red-striped caterpillar shows every sign of being unpalatable and is markedly different in coloration and behaviour from other sphingid caterpillars. It feeds in the open by day, in contrast to most of its relatives, which are nocturnal, cryptic and apparently palatable. Birds are known to eat these caterpillars, and I have watched a big male *Cebus apella* monkey find a large cryptic sphingid and proceed to eat it with obvious pleasure, biting the tough head capsule off and sucking the contents out of the skin. But when these same monkeys find brilliantly patterned sphingids, which often mass on tree trunks, they avoid them and even express what the primatologists who study them describe as alarm calls.

Sometimes, rainforest plants with white sap are not at all toxic. People drink white sap from "milk trees," the name of various *Brosimum* species in the fig family. *Brosimum* trees were among the rainforest trees especially guarded by the Mayas who managed tracts of forest in the Yucatán Peninsula and the Petén region of Guatemala. We make chewing gum out of the milky sap of *Manilkara* trees, the "chicle" trees that were also selectively maintained in Mayan forests. In this case, the sap is still defensive in function, although it works not by chemical damage but by physical obstruction, acting as a gum or glue that makes feeding on it impossible. Rubber is a result of the interaction between a euphorb tree and the herbivores that attempt to breach its bark.

Some arthropods also rely on tacky expulsions for defence. The onychophorans such as *Peripatus*, caterpillarlike animals that patrol the leaf litter of rainforest, are a primitive crossover between annelid worms and arthropods. They are predators on relatively large, mobile prey such as crickets and roaches. Truly peripatetic, onychophorans are no match for a bounding cricket or a flying roach. Instead, they snare their prey with a squirt of proteinaceous glue. These same strands of sticky cement are used to fend off attacking ants.

In some cases, adult insects actually go out and collect defensive compounds from plants. The beautiful ithomiine butterflies gather their defensive compounds as adults rather than as larvae, a somewhat surprising method since ithomiines in the caterpillar stage feed almost exclusively on nightshades. One might expect them to gather defensive compounds from their larval host plants, since nightshades are among the most alkaloid-rich families known, giving us nicotine and many pharmaceutically potent alkaloids and hallucinogens. But for some reason, these butterflies pursue their alkaloids as adults. Ithomiines, especially males, visit various composites and borages whose nectar contains pyrrolizidine alkaloids. Butterfly collectors have long known that one good way to collect masses of male ithomiines is to hang out bunches of dried heliotrope plants rich in these alkaloids. Certain plants, favouring selective and efficient pollination by butterflies, secrete the compounds into their flower nectar, making it repellent to bees, ants and wasps.

Male ithomiines concentrate the alkaloids in patches of scent scales on their upper forewings, which they expose when sitting on a sunny leaf. The courtship function of the scales seems obvious, and females of some related butterflies are known to be attracted by the presence of these alkaloids in male sexual pheromones. Ecologist Bill Haber believes that the alkaloids in the male scent scales may also be the attraction mechanism causing the formation of ithomiine leks, diffuse aggregations

of hundreds of individuals and up to 30 species that fly and display together in the understorey. The fact that the alkaloid-laced butterflies are repellent to birds enhances the value of such aggregation for butterflies which are courting and mating. Each mating lek can be considered a giant Müllerian mimicry complex advertising the toxicity of its members.

In Monteverde, I have visited two such leks in stretches of steep-sided riparian forest. Month after month, the butterflies were there in the same spot. They used a variety of warning colour patterns. Some species were of soft golden translucence; others had bold tiger stripes of orange and black or black and yellow bars. Many were transparent, all but invisible except when their glassy wings were flecked with sunlight. The lek had a languid air. The butterflies circled around and around, indifferent to my presence, delicate and evanescent but unafraid. The males alternately paused spread-eagled on leaves, then flew up in courtship pursuits, only to eddy back with slow, placid wing beats. In their tranquil floating flight was the sign of the protective alkaloid gathered from the bittersweet nectar of flowers.

Perhaps an hour amid such an ithomiine aggregation is the best way to appreciate the virtues of defensive toxins. Such molecules bring not just pain or caution into the naturalist's experience of rainforest. They are the invisible progenitors of great beauty.

As adults, the male ithomiine butterflies (*Callithomia hydra*) collect alkaloids from certain plants in order to initiate leks. These alkaloids have been shown to augment their unpalatability.

EL TIGRE

WHY JAGUARS ARE THE ULTIMATE PREDATOR

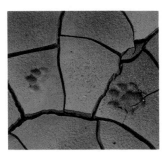

He has coughed in the night outside my tent in Peru, a throaty sound that raises primordial hackles, turns full the heart's pounding throttle and sends a squeeze of adrenaline into the arteries. The ears crackle with reborn awareness of the forest noises outside; the mind wonders if the rustle in the leaf litter is his careful tread. While plodding the muddy pampas in Bolivia, I have stopped and looked around wide-eyed at fresh, wet prints, each as large as my face. But for me, he remains an invisible presence. I have yet to see *el tigre* in the flesh.

Jaguar sign is here and there in Neotropical forest, but *el tigre* is always thinly spread and encountered only by people who are either diligent or lucky. Those who are both have the best chance of all. Yet if the jaguar is glimpsed only sporadically, it is nevertheless perpetually present in the lives of the animals and in the minds and cultures of the people who live in the rainforest.

The largest, most powerful predator in the Neotropical forest, *Panthera onca*, or *Felis onca*, as some systematists call it, lives at the top of the trophic pyramid. The biomass of a single jaguar, weighing up to 160 kilograms, represents the end point for thousands of other lives, from plant to insect and small mammal and bird, fish and reptile, into this final magnificent feline form.

This cat, this spotted panther, is a geographic generalist. The only New World member of the genus *Panthera*, the jaguar ranges all the way from the southwestern

United States to the Argentine. It prowls in coastal rainforest and roams all the way to the edge of the tree line in the Andes. No natural competitor is powerful enough to restrict the foraging excursions of this cat.

What does a jaguar eat? Everything it can. Or so it seems. Mammalogist Louise Emmons, working in Peru, observed that jaguars kill and eat almost any vertebrate they encounter, except perhaps adult tapir, which may be difficult to take down. The tapir's technique for dealing with a jaguar foolish enough to leap aboard is to crash blindly through dense vegetation until a stout limb sweeps the jaguar off. Theodore Roosevelt, who had a fascination for that sort of phenomenon, noted that "the tapir is no respecter of timber."

Jaguars take even white-lipped peccary, in spite of that group's formidable social defence. Herds of white-lips usually number 50 to 100 animals. Compact, powerful creatures with large, slashing teeth, they charge an intruder from all sides when attacked or threatened and could easily wound or kill a cat on the ground. The jaguar's strategy is to wait in a tree for the herd to pass by, quickly drop down upon a single peccary, kill it with a neck bite, then leap back into the tree. Crouching on a branch a mere metre or two above the ground puts the jaguar well beyond the reach of the pigs. The alarmed pigs have nothing to attack, and the jaguar is later able to descend and feed on its prey. If the animal is light enough, the jaguar may carry it into the tree immediately. But white-lip herds are seminomadic and not predictably available prey. The large cat must therefore use other foraging tactics as well.

Game is rarely concentrated in rainforest the way it is at African water holes or around winter deeryards in North America. So the jaguar spends much of its time on the prowl, waiting for random encounters with a great variety of potential prey items. It is one of the few Neotropical mammals that are about equally active day and night, perhaps a reflection of the dietary breadth it requires. Surveying scat samples, Emmons found that jaguars take both diurnal and nocturnal animals, including squirrels, opossums, rodents like paca and capybara, deer, monkeys and birds, as well as grass and something she lists as "unidentified scaly lumps." Only the peccary seems to be taken more often than a random walk would suggest.

Surprise is a crucial element of the hunt and is no doubt the reason the jaguar has a spotted coat that camouflages it in the forest's mottle of light and shade. (There is a rare black form of the jaguar that closely resembles an Asian black panther, a form that would seem well adapted for hunting by night.) The hunting jaguar's task is to see before being seen. In this, it is aided by the large, forward-set eyes typical of the big cats, which give them great depth perception in the range of 15 to 25 metres and stereoscopic

The jaguar (*Felis onca*), left, is the largest terrestrial predator in the New World rainforest. Heavy jaws with a massive set of muscles give it a wide, rounded face, centre, and one of the most powerful bites of any cat. An adult jaguar leaves an unmistakably large paw print, with deep, rounded toe and palm impressions, right.

Jaguars (*Felis onca*) are generalist predators that eat a great variety of animals. Medium-sized mammals such as this coatimundi (*Nasua nasua*), which are common in the rain-forest, are one of the jaguar's dietary mainstays.

vision beyond that, distances that a jaguar can cover in a few quick bounds. The rest is over quickly. Unlike the slightly smaller and more delicate puma with which it coexists, the jaguar has remarkable crushing power in its bite. Its massive skull gives this cat an almost square-headed look — the result of the zygomatic arches of bone that flare out from each side of its head to accommodate the huge muscles running from the anchor site, a large sagittal crest of bone astride the skull. The muscles power a set of heavy jaws equipped with stout canines. Ecologist Richard Kilte has calculated the bite force of the jaguar to be about 150 percent greater than that of a puma and as much as 10 times that of the smaller cats such as margays, which is why the jaguar can eat animals like caimans. Anyone who has grabbed even a tiny live specimen of these strong, durably plated reptiles will recognize that taking such a creature in the mouth and swallowing it ranks as a notable gastronomic accomplishment.

The jaguar is a water-loving cat and catches a considerable portion of its food there. Emmons radio-collared and tracked jaguars and found that they spent much time hunting along the river's edge, where they would snag, wrestle, kill and eat resting caimans. The jaguar is also reported by other observers to fish for tambaqui, a large characoid piranha that eats fruit, by taking up a post on a limb over the water and tapping on the surface in imitation of falling fruit. When the fish rises to investigate,

the cat snags it with its claws. This aquatic preference and the jaguar's ability to feed on tough prey appear to be the major differences between jaguars and pumas.

Reptiles such as turtles and crocodiles were once an abundant resource in Amazonia and the Orinoco drainage; the sandbars and beaches used to swarm with nesting *Podocnemis* turtles. Humboldt wrote about the turtle nestings that produced millions of eggs — so many, in fact, that the harvests which used to sustain both Indians and jaguars were taken over by the Jesuit and Franciscan missionaries. They massed the eggs in dugouts, boiled off the oil and exported the resulting *manteca de tortugas*, or turtle lard, to Europe, consuming in the process some 33 million eggs annually from one section of the Orinoco. Predictably, the turtle populations are now devastated, but Humboldt recorded that "a great number of these animals are devoured by jaguars the moment they leave the water" and was disconcerted to find that not even fires would keep the jaguars away from his campsites along the turtle beaches. He noted that in order to devour the turtles at their ease, the jaguars "turn them so that the under shell is uppermost. In this situation, the turtles cannot rise; and as the jaguar turns many more than he can eat in one night, the Indians often avail themselves of his cunning and avidity."

Although the jaguar is able to use its long claws and paws to pull a river turtle from its shell, access to much of the reptilian resource depends on the jaguar's uniquely powerful bite. The most impressive evidence of the jaguar's jaw power I have seen is in its handling of the land tortoise's shell.

Around the area where Emmons worked at Cocha Cashu in Peru's Manú Biosphere Reserve, there is a healthy population of the ground-dwelling tortoise *Geochelone denticulata*. This tortoise is hefty, weighing about 4.4 kilograms. Its protective plastron and carapace are solid bone that appears sturdy enough to resist an attack with a hammer. But on my first visit to Cocha Cashu, I was surprised to see a huge pile of partially demolished *Geochelone* shells. The pile had been collected by biolo-

gists working in the area. The shells, which are about as long as a football, invariably looked as though they had been treated like a huge, armour-plated hamburger, with the jaguar simply taking the shell in its mouth and biting right through the side of it with what must be a tremendous bone-cracking, shell-splintering crunch. One inevitably concludes that a jaguar would find the human skull about as challenging as a ripe cantaloupe. For its size, no cat bites harder than *el tigre*.

Panthera onca is a creature with a reputation for possessing little fear of humans. Records of attacks on humans are numerous. The Jesuit missionary Eder, who wrote of life in eastern Bolivia in the years prior to 1772, had enough information at hand to give a detailed chronology of the way in which a jaguar dispatches humans, beginning with an attack to the head, followed by consumption of the throat region and great attention to the consequent outpouring of blood from the large arteries, which it carefully licked up "in order not to lose a single drop." (This is an approach that all the big cats seem to use when taking down prey large enough to require a suffocating throat bite rather than a severing bite to the back of the neck.) Perhaps that fearlessness and power to threaten, coupled with the role of top predator which it shares with humans of the rainforest, explain the jaguar's dominant presence in the mythology of the forest tribes of Central and South America.

Anthropologist Janet Suskind explains the anthropomorphic appeal the jaguar holds for the Sharanahua of Brazil and Peru: "Ordinary game was taken with bows and arrows, but men and jaguars were killed with spears. Jaguars, like men, are predators, the only important predators in the tropical forest. In a real sense, jaguars are competitors for meat . . . because he is a competitor, the jaguar, like all strangers, is dangerous and should be killed before he attacks." So, too, the Desana of Colombia recognize the ecological role of the jaguar. Of all the animals in the forest, only the jaguar is not subservient to the spiritual "master of the animals." Instead, it is acclaimed as a resourceful hunter and is represented symbolically as "a fertilizing force derived directly from the sun."

When Amazonian Indians use hallucinogenic vehicles to explore and divine fate and the future, they often rendezvous with *el tigre*. Manuel Cordova, a native Peruvian, describes how under the influence of ayahuasca, or yage (the extract of *Banisteriopsis* vines), visits with jaguars, sometimes black ones, were traditional: "My sensing faculties became those of the black animals. Sight, sound, smell, feel and instinct were tuned in with those of this most astute beast of the forest. And we prowled together — investigating dark, hidden things beyond the ken of uninitiated man, unexplainable in his language." Ethnobotanist Richard Evans Schultes, who lived with

Many carnivorous mammals are active primarily at night. *Felis onca*, however, hunts both night and day in pursuit of such animals as agoutis, peccaries and certain monkeys that are also active during the daytime. Its spotted coat provides camouflage in the mottled sun and shade of the rainforest understorey through which it moves.

139

Amazonian Indians and explored their hallucinogenic rituals, writes that along with snakes, jaguars dominate the visions, "since they are the only beings respected and feared by the Indians of the tropical forest; because of their power and stealth, they have assumed a place of primacy in aboriginal religious beliefs. In many tribes, the shaman becomes a feline during the intoxication, exercising his powers as a cat." The relationship is reflected in the fact that in many Indian languages, the same word is used to mean shaman and jaguar.

Jaguar cults abound in pre-Columbian Neotropical culture from Mexico south to Brazil. In the most remote forests of Amazonia, where shotguns have not replaced spears, necklaces of jaguar claws and teeth remain the hunter's emblem of valour. Many of these cultures are now extinct, but the jaguar's face continues to stare out from carvings, friezes and glyphs on temples in Mexico and along the Peruvian coastal desert. A jaguar stalks in a highly stylized way across a Chorotega Indian ceramic I bought, a newly made piece sold along a paved highway in Costa Rica. The Olmecs, Zapotecs, Aztecs, Mayas, Chavíns and Incas all gave *el tigre* a place at the top of their spiritual pantheon of gods.

But where is the jaguar's place now in the cultures of Latin America? Humans, the competitors and predators of jaguars, have succeeded in reducing their numbers throughout most of the jaguar's natural range. It is easy

for an animal that roams over areas as large as 6,500 hectares to run out of room. In Monteverde, Costa Rica, jaguars have rebounded following increased protection of forest and wildlife. But the forest that remains is a ragged island which is only 100,000 or so hectares in area. All around it are cattle and dairy farms. The killing of cattle by jaguars is on the increase.

In Monteverde, the local conservation league where I sometimes work was notified by forest guards and farmers about three incidents of jaguar attacks that destroyed a bull, a cow and a horse, all in different localities. We did not know how many jaguars were involved, but we knew that if nothing else were done, the farmers' reaction would be to run dogs on the jaguars, tree the wild cats and shoot them. Because the jaguar population was limited to perhaps 5 to 20 individuals, we decided to compensate the farmers for their losses in return for their agreement not to kill the offending jaguars should they show themselves. The money could have been used to protect more habitat, but that protection would have been at the cost of jaguar lives. The only alternative was to try to locate and tranquillize the jaguars and move them to a new site. Few people have the skill to manage such an operation without considerable risk to the animals. But our greatest problem was not technology; it was space. Officials at several nearby national parks refused to accommodate any jaguars. They, too, were running at capacity, and moving animals around is one way to spread disease. In fact, Costa Rica has almost run out of habitat that might absorb *el tigre*.

In countries such as Costa Rica, jaguars may be among what tropical ecologist Dan Janzen calls "the living dead," animals whose needs for space are so great that their populations are already too small and too thinly spread. Although they still exist, the living dead are irrevocably headed for extinction in those areas which lack the huge amounts of land needed to sustain genetically viable, non-inbred populations.

It is an understandable temptation to give up on something that is labelled a member of the living dead. But the concept should do more than simply allow us to relegate animals such as the jaguar to the category of extinction and to focus our attention on less demanding species. Instead, it highlights the necessity of fighting hardest for those areas which are still large enough to sustain the jaguar in its natural state. These cats are what is known as an umbrella species. With their popular appeal, they are able to attract strong public support, and if enough space is saved for the jaguar, a huge amount of habitat for the lower echelons of living creatures is also guaranteed. And only a system like this contains the true ecological character and full complement of rainforest.

Jaguars and other cats such as ocelots are "keystone predators." This means that one of the functions they perform is the regulation of the abundance of some of the more prolific rodents. There is a dichotomy in the reproductive rates of rainforest mammals. Many herbivorous mammals, especially seed-eating rodents like agoutis, peccaries and capybaras, have large litters. The small rodents are even more fecund. Emmons has found that ocelots, for example, cropped these small rodents at a correspondingly tremendous rate, removing 69 percent of the annual production, while jaguars consumed peccaries, coatimundis, capybaras and others in proportion to their abundance and at a much lower rate overall.

Ecologist John Terborgh suggests that these two predators have a strong regulating effect because they have either a high cropping rate, as in the case of ocelots, or one that is tied to prey abundance—that is, the most numerous animals are those most frequently eaten by jaguars. He found support for this thesis when he compared densities of these herbivores in areas of Peru, where the cat populations remain healthy, with those in areas like Panama, where cats have been annihilated. In Panama, incidentally, the well-studied field site Barro Colorado Island has elevated levels of opossums, armadillos and rabbits and has 10 times as many animals such as agoutis and coatimundis as do the areas that retain large predator populations. In other words, removal of the top-level predators did not cause the collapse of the trophic pyramid. But it did result in a major shift in proportions, destroying communities of common herbivore species such as the rodents.

The eventual outcome of this shift is not easy to predict, because the effects may not be evident for a century. For example, agouti and peccary abundance may destroy the ability of palm trees to reseed, thereby reducing the recruitment of young palm seedlings into the forest. In addition to sustaining important food animals such as peccaries, macaws and rodents, palms are keystone resources for the indigenous people of Amazonia. Of all plants, the palm family is universally rated as the most important, being a source of oils, fruits rich in vitamins, high-protein nuts, fibre and waterproof thatching for houses and the best wood for bows and arrows. Fewer cats means more agoutis, which means fewer palms, which in turn means fewer peccaries and even fewer cats. If the interaction continues long enough, we lose the cats, but ultimately, the palms might go as well, followed by the agoutis and peccaries. The symbolic importance of the jaguar in mythic lore may be more vital and appropriate than we will ever realize.

Jaguars themselves have no predators other than humans; before the advent of guns, they were abundant. But despite their appeal, jaguars are still being killed at great rates. During zoologist Alan Rabinowitz's two-year study of jaguars in Belize, all six of his study animals died. But pristine jaguar populations can still be found.

The last time I was in Manú, I saw a jaguar skull someone had picked up in the forest. The animal had apparently died of old age, its teeth worn down to mere stubs; perhaps it spent its last days searching for snakes, fish and other easily swallowed prey. One might find such a prospect a bit grim and sad, but I did not. That skull was concrete evidence of something magnificent: a place where a jaguar can grow old enough to wear down its powerful teeth, where a jaguar can hunt and not be hunted, where a jaguar can walk its way across its full life span, the measure given freely before the age of guns, poachers and fur traders. As the days of the living dead dawn in more and more countries, we must treasure those places where this regal cat can still lie down to die, possessed of all its allotted days. In such a place, I can wait patiently for my chance to see a jaguar. As long as *el tigre* walks, the spirit of wilderness remains in the forest.

Jaguar populations are declining in part because the attractive spotted pelt of this cat is still widely sought by poachers. But loss of adequate habitat is the greatest threat to the survival of this wide-ranging predator.

BEYOND THE GUN

A JOURNEY INTO VIRGIN AMAZONIA

My companions on a journey made in the late 1980s to Manú, the largest national park on Earth, were a typically ragged-looking handful of field biologists — a mix of Peruvians, Princetonians and Canadians. We left the high altitudes of Cuzco, Peru, in a truck loaded with the several tonnes of paraphernalia necessary for a trip into tropical rainforest — giant hooks for catfish, small ones for piranha, thousands of crackers in airtight tins, drums of kerosene, kayaks and beer — and headed toward one of the few truly pristine regions of the Tropics, a trackless land where the wildlife roams unhunted and Stone Age humans still live free in the untamed vastness of eastern Amazonia. It was an experience that completely altered my understanding of the well-worn phrase "virgin forest."

Manú sprawls over the southeastern corner of Peru, running from the edge of the cold altiplano high above the tree line, dropping 3,500 metres across the slopes of the Andes and spreading into the Amazonian lowlands. It is now officially designated as Manú Biosphere Reserve, a protected area that encompasses 1.8 million hectares. The great area harbours more than 1,000 bird species, 1,500 kinds of plant and over 200 types of mammal, including 13 species of monkey. Manú is probably the most biologically diverse preserve on Earth, and much of the park is still a biological *terra incognita*.

As our truck crawled up the serpentine mountain road,

I began to understand why Manú remains a new, unspoiled world. Intimidating chasms began yawning below the truck soon after we left the Sacred Valley of the Incas and headed over the eastern flank of the Andes. The road was a one-way affair, a narrow slice with barely an inch for human error and too slender to permit two-way traffic. Instead, travel reverses direction every second day.

Much of the single lane was hemmed in on one side by jagged rock walls and on the other by empty sky. Nevertheless, Andean truckers make the most of gravity. Condemned to crawl up steep slopes, they compensate when going downhill, sending their heavily loaded, bald-tired charges careening around blind hairpin turns, accompanied by whining brakes and muttered appeals to Providence from the riders. Often, the drivers fortify themselves against the cold and chasms with an excess of that potent alcoholic hooch Peruvians call *pisco*.

Unfortunately, the one-way rule is often bent. There is always some maniac in a hurry, with a bribe for the guard at the road entrance and a willingness to risk his life and the lives of others to make the trip in the wrong direction. One such reprobate came looming out of the dusk at us. Luckily, there was room to back up, pull over and allow him to go on into the dark against the grain.

At one point, I saw the sobering roadside crosses that mark the failures of the system. Leaning out over the side of the truck and staring down into the late-afternoon shadows, I could see, hundreds of metres below on the rocks, a splattering of truck doors, wheels and debris. And I had heard that the park service had recently lost a truck and two men who had dropped over the side farther ahead on the road, a fact which one tried mentally to bury but which resurfaced with every lurching curve.

Alpacas, peasants walking barefoot on the cold, stony soil and the great sweep of the tussock grass marked our passage above the 4,000-metre level. High in the treeless altiplano, the first boundary marker of the park appeared as dusk came on. The sky turned from a deep purple to a night sky so cold and clear and black that it felt as if we had passed along the very edge of the atmosphere and into space. A retreat into sleeping bags, and sleep was on. Hours later, I awoke with a face wet from the mist, and we began our descent into the zone of moss-festooned cloud forest.

Even in the gloom, I could see that the cloud forest remained intact, a welcome contrast to much of the Andes where the land has been cleared for coca plantations. Andean cloud-forest plants are distinguished by one of the world's highest degrees of endemism, the localized occurrence of unique species. Often, each set of ridges supports many plants that grow there and nowhere else. The densely matted, damp tangle of habitat, a zone Peruvians refer to as the *ceja de montana*, the eyebrows of the mountains, is home to little-known wildlife. Spectacled bears

Flocks of the blue and gold macaw (*Ara ararauna*), left, require hundreds of square kilometres of forest, while insects such as tortoise beetles of the Chrysomelidae family, centre, may survive in a few hectares. The wire-tailed manakin (*Pipra filicauda*), right, is intermediate in its spatial demands. Retaining the wilderness ecosystems that still harbour the full range of rainforest organisms is an urgent scientific priority.

143

Much of Amazonian rainforest is accessible only by river. The remote backwaters, beyond the reach of motorized transport, logging roads and the market economy, remain a haven for ecologically vulnerable species such as giant river otters (*Pteronura brasiliensis*) and the last refuge of the indigenous human inhabitants of tropical rainforest.

climb and clamber here, pulling bromeliads from branches to eat. The cow-sized, woolly-coated mountain tapir, completely unstudied in spite of its bulk, travels deeply rutted trails and centuries-old routes along ridges beyond human penetration.

At midnight, we stopped for food and bladder relief in an isolated hamlet, the one-shack town of Piowata. We sat on benches and listened as a battery-powered radio blasted out the rhythmic and appropriately mournful *huayno* music of the Andes. Red-eyed guinea pigs scurried nervously underfoot, as if anticipating that they would soon be the next feature on the menu. John Terborgh, the Princeton ecologist and Manú veteran who had planned the trip, could finally relax. His huge, broad smile gleamed in the lantern light as he looked around and exclaimed, "This is the real Peru."

To many North Americans, the real Peru is an Andean tragedy, a place of agricultural landscapes, deserts and mountains, a worn-out country that has seen the Inca civilization replaced by tragic combinations: the lucrative cocaine trade mixed with utter poverty, guerrilla warfare and militarism, great resources and great waste. We had seen all of that in Cuzco and Lima—in machine-gun-toting police on every corner, in the newspapers' daily chronicle of violence, in the blood-red political slogans of hate on every street and in the squalid alleys lined by adobe walls capped with broken bottles. But beyond the

coastal cities, beyond the heavily settled Andean plateaus, there are still small, simple villages and, beyond them, Amazonian wilderness. The real Peru for a biologist is that land still free from the pressing density of humanity.

Madre de Dios province, where the park is located, has only one inhabitant per 100 hectares, and most people are found in the town of Puerto Maldonado, near the Brazilian-Bolivian border. Yet true wilderness is not easily found even in this part of Peru. "Much of Amazonia," says Terborgh, "is a hollow shell as far as the animals are concerned. The forest is there, but hunters and trappers have bagged the big cats, the monkeys, the macaws, the caimans and the giant otters." Manú is an exception, one of the few places where one can study ecological communities that are unaltered by human influence. The heart of Manú re-creates the time when gunshot blasts or even the puffing of blowguns and the twang of bowstrings were unknown sounds to the parrots, monkeys, tapirs and peccaries.

To get beyond the range of the shotgun takes almost a week of travel. Terborgh and others like him make the trip out of necessity. As I had learned on the mountain roads, the journey is filled with hazards and difficulties. Terborgh and his students have had boats full of gear stolen; trees have crashed down on them, sinking them in awkward circumstances; and leishmaniasis, a fly-transmitted microorganism that eats hideous leprosylike ulcers in one's anatomy, has infected Terborgh several times. Leishmaniasis ulcers appear unpredictably, often months after exposure, erupting anywhere on the body. They grow steadily larger if left untreated. A month-long series of injections with antimony compounds is required to halt the microorganism's progress. The treatment strains the liver, tires the victim and makes the joints ache, and even when vanquished, leishmaniasis often leaves a legacy of disfiguring scars. In Cuzco, we had seen many destitute Indians with noses and faces eaten away by the disease.

We entered the lowlands, and the road, a rocky bed built up during an era of unsuccessful oil exploration, became hemmed in with vegetation. The song of an un-described species of antbird caught Terborgh's attention, and we scanned the trees for a glimpse of it, all the while trying to duck out of the reach of the dangling hooked lengths of bamboo brushing over the truck. On one trip, Terborgh's ear was torn in two by the once graceful limbs. Nevertheless, we were all gaping at the rich lowland flora as we passed by. As we rolled hour after hour through forest, we did not see a solitary monkey or mammal of any kind. No macaws brightened the sky.

The first European explorers of the New World Tropics invariably made similar observations on the scarcity of game. Historian William Prescott, writing about the con-quest of Peru, summed up the conquistadors' impression of the "funereal forests," stating that "even brute creation appeared instinctively to have shunned the spot, and nei-ther beast nor bird was seen by the wanderers." Cornel Whiffen, explorer of the northwest Amazon, echoed these remarks, as did Henry Bates and other naturalists before him. The trip, like most others I had made to tropical for-ests, was so far confirming the impression that animal populations are relatively low in tropical rainforests. I was to change my mind a few days later.

By midmorning, we had successfully forded the Rio Carbon and had reached the end of the road at Shin-tuya, a village of acculturated Indians. We watched gold miners buying supplies, a couple of trucks taking on squared-off mahogany logs and the usual cadre of gaunt dogs and swine half-heartedly prospecting for garbage and human excrement.

Our highway was now the Rio Alto Madre de Dios, a river whose name might read majestically as the Upper River of the Mother of God. The Alto Madre proved to be a braided, gravelly propellant, spilling cold and clear out of the mountains and running swiftly over the rocky bars, swerving around islands of flood-swept trees and debris. Our craft, a narrow wooden boat of *Cedrela* planks, made rapid time, slithering past the sunken trees and scraping over boulders. My expectations began to rise as we saw flocks of blue-green parakeets swirl like clouds of coordinated living confetti, and from time to time, blue

and gold macaws passed in pairs overhead. By nightfall, we reached the confluence of the Manú River, a typically sluggish, yellow-brown Amazonian river that we would ascend for two days.

Before the sun has fully risen, there are two glorious hours of pale rose and then yellow-tinted light, when the mist trails in wisps and eddies along the water and wild-life still lurks and stalks and sings along the banks and

A rufescent tiger-heron (*Tigrisoma lineatum*) hunts in solitude along the shore of a lake in Peru's Manú National Park, one of the largest protected wilder-ness areas on Earth.

beaches. But as soon as the sun climbs above the treetops, the water glares painfully, like a rippling mirror, ever shifting to catch and force your eyes away. The landscape of forest, bank and beach is bleached to flat greens, washed-out browns and white. Joseph Conrad, who trav-elled the rivers of Southeast Asia, wrote of "the monot-ony of the inanimate brooding sunshine of the Tropics," and it is true that under its brilliance, much of the wild-life wilts away into the shady forest interior.

The traveller's boat, as often as not, is powered by a belching diesel or, on the smaller tributaries, by a thump-ing *peque-peque*, the onomatopoeic name for a con-traption consisting of a 16-horsepower 4-cycle motor driving an improvised shaft that protrudes far back be-hind the boat. A craft thus powered makes only modest progress as it zigzags back and forth, working up the sinuous path of the river. The pace of travel is somno-lent, the green wall of vegetation is mute, save for the narcotic whine and drone of cicadas, and it is rarely long before a number of devotedly sanguinary black-flies pick up the scent of the captive passengers and crew. Under such circumstances, the veteran of tropical river travel often pulls a hat over the face and hunkers down, retreating into torpidity.

At the guard post controlling access to the interior of the park, we were surprised to encounter a group of Yora Indians, one of several tribes that find refuge in Manú.

Amazonia's rainforest is the most diverse of all tropical forests. A few square kilometres may harbour as many as 500 species of bird, 80 varieties of frog and several hundred tree species. Vast areas of unbroken Amazonian forest still remain.

The area has an ethnic diversity that matches its biological diversity. Piro, Machiguenga, Yora, Amahuaca, Campa, Huachipari, Masco-Piro, Amarakaeri and other tribes live in or around the park. Some, like the Yora, have only recently been contacted, while others, like the Masco-Piro, have wisely remained in a Stone Age state.

The Yora we met were on their way downriver for some purpose we could not divine; no park guard speaks their particular Panoan dialect. Perhaps it was their new discovery of fishhooks or of the use of clothes as protection against the biting sandflies that had brought them out of the remote end of the park. The males wore their penises cinched and tied up with cords around their waists. Some were adorned with strings of beads that encircled their faces and were joined to the septums of their noses. Something about their gesticulations made them look unmistakably wild. They are, indeed, a fierce tribe, willing to unleash mighty two-metre-long arrows at other Indians, oil explorers and lumber prospectors alike. In recent times, they have been gradually encroaching upon the territory of the Machiguenga, one of the other ethnic groups of the area. Only in the past two years have the Yora made peaceful contact with anthropologists and the missionaries who haunt all tropical wilderness areas, hoping to gather souls no matter what the cultural cost.

Such religious zeal has also had an ecological downside. Before the park was created, the missionaries funded their proselytizing by running a poaching and animal-hide-export business using Indian labour. The Indian culture, along with the wildlife, was being systematically destroyed until the park service expelled the missionaries and decreed a hands-off policy with regard to the indigenous peoples of Manú. The Indians are now free to live in a traditional manner in the distant reaches of the park. Biologists and all other visitors are forbidden to contact indigenous peoples in order that neither their health nor their cultural equilibrium is imperilled. Nevertheless, we could not avoid the encounter with the Yora, and we took away from it a deeper appreciation of the park and the sanctuary it offers the wildest and most endangered organism: aboriginal humanity. We felt the strangeness of meeting fellow humans who still hunt and fight with bows and arrows, have no conception of what a park is and do not know what Peru means.

The first night on the river, we camped on a sandbar and had tuna and crackers for supper, items that became dietary staples. A *friaje* wind from the south blew damp, cold air, and the warmer river steamed. As we battled the unexpectedly low temperatures with a bottle of ouzo, Terborgh recounted a story about one of his research trips to New Guinea. After travelling with a group of porters far into the highlands, Terborgh and fellow ecologist Jared Diamond trudged into camp near a remote village. Terborgh sat down and pulled off his boots. To his amazement, the simple act sent a swarm of onlooking villagers running into the forest shrieking with fright. One of the more worldly porters explained to the mystified Terborgh: "Them bush kanakas thought you pulling off your feet." The vulnerability of such people cannot be overestimated, and the park plays an important role in thwarting the rapacious tendrils of civilization that first reach into the frontier — gold miners, loggers, coca traffickers, missionaries and miscellaneous hucksters — and often sponge up profits at the expense of the ancestral inhabitants of the forest.

Ironically, part of the value of the park comes from one of the past incursions into the Manú region. Local accounts and limited historical observations suggest that during the rubber boom which began a century ago, the Manú Indians were ravaged by the ruthless Peruvian rubber baron Carlos Fitzcarraldo. In his battle for rubber territory and in opening a route to the Rio Alto Madre de Dios, Fitzcarraldo decimated the Masco Indian tribes that once lived along the Manú River. Piro Indians were employed to enslave other Indians as labour for rubber tapping. Those who resisted were killed; many others succumbed to epidemics of infectious disease. The rubber boom was short-lived, and the traffic of tappers and the strife they caused ceased at the turn of the century. But the Indian population, impoverished as it is and lacking the most basic health care, has not rebounded, and today, there are regions of the park that are emptier than they have been for thousands of years. The depopulated portion of the park is now as close as one can get to the Amazon as it was before any human settlement occurred. Biologists base their work in the depopulated area because the animal communities live in a state as free from human intervention as one can find anywhere.

After two days on the Manú, we pulled up at a beach and began carrying the gear several hundred metres into Cocha Cashu, the field site. The Cocha is a cashew-shaped lake, an old oxbow left by one of the shifts in the meandering river. Greenly productive, it resembles a giant, curving trough of pea soup. Our encampment was on floodplain soil, relatively rich alluvial silt that supports the classic, yet rarely encountered, high rainforest. The biggest trees were truly huge, with buttresses as wide as 10 metres from side to side. Lianas as thick as the largest ship cables crawled upward to a canopy 60 to 70 metres high. The trees were festooned with strange flowers, some like pink powder puffs erupting from the trunks.

I pitched my tent at the lake edge and awaited my first night in this forest. Promptly at 6 o'clock, darkness seeped in like tea, filtering around the trees. Huge click beetles with luminous eye spots shining the cool, fluorescent green light of fireflies streaked through the dusk. Night came not as dark emptiness but as a rising cloud of living sound. Thousands of nameless voices broke out, and

katydids and crickets began to file their legs and wing combs. They had the percussive, metallic sounds of tambourines, the rhythm of ratchets and castanets. They entered into choruses of trills and reverberations which had the quality of the radio signals that come echoing in from deep space as you dial the shortwave radio searching for the news of the world. Over the lake, noisy with flopping fish, where the sky was revealed, the Southern Cross lay on its side beside the Milky Way, that luminous flow of stars the native Amazonians call "the River."

As the crescent moon emerged, a strange call resounded nearby, a loud, vomiting *boorkk* that could only be the giant potoo, a night-active bird that bears a remarkable resemblance to the weathered grey ends of the dead snags on which it perches. With its superb camouflage, it was impossible to pick out even with a flashlight. The retching voice issuing invisibly from a spot right above was ominous. Perhaps that is why Peruvians believe the call is a bad omen and have named the bird *ayamama*, a Quechua word meaning "mother of the cadaver." But the bird ceased calling, and I drifted off to sleep under a rain of chittering cries and bits of debris that accompanied a family of night monkeys foraging by the light of the stars and the moon.

In the morning, I awoke with a jolt of adrenaline stimulated by the creaking, tearing sound of a massive tree limb breaking overhead. I scrambled out but saw no sign of impending doom. At breakfast, Cocha Cashu veterans informed me that the sound was nothing more than the display of a piping guan that uses its wing feathers to create the distinctive call. It was a sound I would hear with unusual regularity. Around Cocha Cashu, guans proved to be more abundant than I have seen anywhere else in the New World Tropics. Big, meaty birds that usually have a small clutch, they are among the first elements of the avifauna to vanish under hunting pressure. Whenever

Tapirs (*Tapirus terrestris*) are the largest terrestrial mammal found in New World rainforest. Prized for their meat, they are often hunted to extinction around areas of dense human settlement. Parks such as Manú, which sustain small numbers of indigenous inhabitants who traditionally hunt for subsistence needs, are able to maintain healthy tapir populations.

The spix's guan (*Penelope jacquacu*), resting at its midday roost in Manú National Park, is a favourite game bird because of its large size, high-quality meat and the relative ease with which it can be shot. With a low reproductive rate, guans disappear rapidly under hunting pressure, and many populations have been extinguished.

I flush a guan, I am always amazed by the apparent naïveté of the bird. After its brief, noisy alarm reaction when it flaps and hops up from the ground, its strongest impulse seems to be to get a good look at you from a convenient perch. It makes a target that is hard to miss. But here, it was common to see guans in the forest. I often hiked behind a flock of waddling trumpeters, goose-sized fruit-eating birds that bobbed their white rumps nonchalantly as they foraged just a pace or two ahead, and everywhere, plump tinamous scurried along the trails. It was a novel pleasure to have all these big game birds almost underfoot and to hear their songs sung and whistled in strong choruses.

Other animals I had always thought were naturally rare turned out to be present in great numbers. At Cocha Cashu, black spider monkeys, a favoured food throughout the Amazon, were not just common, they were brazen, rattling the branches and chucking debris down on me whenever I disturbed them as they fed in a fig tree. The creek beds were churned and muddied by tapirs on their foraging rounds. On the beach, I saw the tracks of the capybara, the largest rodent in the world (68 kilograms), closely followed by a set of jaguar tracks.

Giant otters are another hallmark of Manú's fauna. Prized for their skin, they have been hunted to the brink of extinction. These two-metre-long, 32-kilogram members of the weasel family need space in which to roam and fish. They travel widely from lake to lake along rivers in groups of four to six adults. Martha Brecht Munn, an ecologist who studied giant otters at Manú, found that each animal eats more than one large fish every hour and that the giant otters will kill anacondas three metres long, attack adult black caimans and even charge a jaguar if it prowls too close. In concert, they are among the planet's most formidable and ecologically demanding predators. So great are the dietary and spatial requirements of the giant otter that Manú probably supports only 100 adults. It takes but a single hide hunter to eliminate a population.

The importance of hunting impressed me most deeply when a Machiguenga, a person born and bred in the Peru-

vian forest, stopped on his way downriver to catch some fish at the Cocha. He hunted with a bow and arrow from a precarious position in a dugout canoe, a thin, tippy proposition under the best of conditions. But he stood erect at the end of the canoe, one foot ahead of the other, a balancing act supreme. He poled himself ahead easily, smoothly, using his two-metre-long bow of black chonta palm. Through my binoculars from the far shore, I could see him staring at the opaque green surface of the lake. Then he nocked an arrow and let it fly. The arrow bobbed up with a thrashing silver bocachica fish impaled on it.

After witnessing that display of skill, I left to do my fieldwork in the forest interior, but Peruvian ornithologist Walter Wurst stayed on to watch the Machiguenga. He shot 20 times and came up with 20 bocachica. Later, Wurst and I learned firsthand just what a mysterious art we had witnessed. Naïvely, we rounded up a bow and some arrows and set out on a similar mission. I paddled, and Wurst knelt in the bow ready to harvest our supper. We were utterly defeated by the wily bocachica. It was not just that Wurst was not as fine a marksman or that my paddle strokes were less smooth than the Machiguenga's. Our difficulties were far more fundamental: the bocachica were completely invisible to us. Long before we could read some sign of their presence, perhaps a bubble rising to the surface, they swirled away. The Machiguenga, having grown up with a bow in his hand and spurred on by absolute necessity, had developed a high level of skill that was not only impressive to us but also completely beyond our perceptual abilities.

Tales of Amazonian Indian hunting skills and woodcraft are legion, but this was the first time I had seen such skill so directly translated into hunting success. That man with a rifle and a few friends could decimate wildlife populations with ease if encouraged by the market economy for illegal hides and wild game. Studies in Peru show that a family of settlers, although lacking the great skills of the indigenous people, consumes about 900 kilograms of monkeys, macaws and other game annually. Little wonder, then, that rainforest game soon grows scarce in the presence of humans. I began to realize the importance for the surviving tribes of Manú of the depopulated areas, which act as a generating space that replenishes the depleted game populations around the villages. Instead of the territorial no-man's-land which warfare imposes, the unpopulated area of the park ensures that game populations will continue to be present as long as a large core remains unhunted.

And in Manú, I began to appreciate why animals that seem common elsewhere — small rodents, sloths, opossums — appeared to be scarcer. Terborgh suggests that in Manú, where there are still all the cats, bush dogs and harpy eagles to keep a close check on them, populations have a more natural balance of numbers than in most

other areas now being studied. Here, limber-limbed spider monkeys leapt wildly through the treetops, and the streams were heavily marked with tapir tracks. I heard, for the first time, the *cough-cough* call of the jaguar at night. Macaws, the glorious parrots I had thought to be rare, settled in abundance in the treetops at dawn to gather the first warm rays of light with their brilliant plumage. The lake was jammed with fish, turtles and caimans.

The significance of such sights was not merely in their beauty. They were a lesson explaining just how limited is our understanding of ecological communities in the Tropics. After 19 years of visiting the Tropics, I thought I had a fair idea of the basic composition of tropical ecological communities. But I was more ignorant than I could have imagined.

Such ignorance is common among ecologists, because tropical biology is concentrated in just a few convenient sites in Costa Rica, Panama and other accessible areas. Almost without exception, the sites are extremely disturbed; their large predator populations and important game species have been radically thinned or eliminated, producing changes we hardly understand. For example, white-lipped peccaries, a social species of pig that requires great expanses of forest habitat, are absent from much of their former range. White-lips are not only major predators but also dispersers of palm seeds, consumers of snakes and tillers of the soil, and their absence must set

off a chain reaction about which we know nothing. As a consequence, what little we do know about tropical ecology is often a biased misimpression. The really significant places go unstudied and are frequently lost to logging and hunting before they are ever known. Terborgh wants to change this. He and his colleagues and students are busy studying the monkeys, macaws, cats, otters and caimans that have vanished from other parts of Amazonia. But Terborgh also has a dream and a plan that embraces more than just Manú. It is to find the funds required to study 10 virgin tropical-forest sites around the world. He sees it as a last-ditch effort to collect the baseline data needed to understand what natural tropical-forest ecosystems are really like before they are irretrievably changed.

One senses his desperation when he writes, "I feel as an astronomer might on being told that the stars were going to burn out in 10 years and that there would only be that long to unravel the mysteries of the heavens."

The stars will wait for as long as we may need to grasp their greatness. But Manú, for all its vastness, has a uniqueness that cannot be taken for granted. If we lose this place and the few others like it, all we will retain are the first few preliminary measurements of our ignorance. We will have lost those special places, the true wilderness where biological mystery breathes and grows inviolate, where the firmament of living species still stands unbroken.

The oxbow lakes of Manú National Park are shallow, nutrient-rich and highly productive aquatic ecosystems. When used at low intensity by indigenous inhabitants, they provide an abundance of protein while sustaining healthy populations of black caiman, giant otter, waterfowl and fish.

FURTHER READING

Writings on the natural history of tropical rainforest are vast and fragmented. Where to begin? The early works of natural history remain among the most informative because of their scope. Above all, they express the sense of discovery that all naturalists experience when making their first contact with tropical rainforest. I recommend the following books that focus on the Neotropics:

Bates, H.W. *The Naturalist on the River Amazons*. London: John Murray, 1864; reprinted Berkeley: University of California Press, 1962.

Belt, T. *The Naturalist in Nicaragua*. London: 1874; reprinted Chicago: University of Chicago Press, 1985, with a foreword by Daniel H. Janzen.

Spruce, R. *Notes of a Botanist on the Amazon and Andes*, 2 vols., edited by A.R. Wallace. London: Macmillan, 1908; reprinted New York: Johnson Reprints, 1970.

Von Humboldt, A. *Personal Narrative of Travels to the Equinoctial Regions of America*, 3 vols. London: G. Rutledge, 1851.

Wallace, A.R. *A Narrative of Travels on the Amazon and Rio Negro*. London: Ward, Lock and Co., 1889; reprinted New York: Dover, 1972.

Wallace, A.R. *Natural Selection and Tropical Nature*. London: Macmillan, 1895.

Waterton, C. *Wanderings in South America*. London: Century Publishing, 1825; reprinted London: Century Publishing, 1983.

In the 20th century, a few biologists have continued the narrative tradition. Books I recommend include:

Beebe, W. *Edge of the Jungle*. New York: Henry Holt, 1921.

Carr, A.F. *High Jungles and Low*. Gainesville: University of Florida Press, 1953.

Skutch, A.F. *A Naturalist in Costa Rica*. Gainesville: University of Florida Press, 1971.

Skutch, A.F. *A Naturalist on a Tropical Farm*. Berkeley: University of California Press, 1980.

Most research on tropical ecology is now published on a piecemeal basis in technical scientific journals such as *Biotropica* or *Journal of Tropical Ecology* and in equally specialized books. The academic system does not reward scientists for producing popular accounts of their research, so books that communicate the experience of rainforest are not being produced by the people who know the most about this environment. There are, however, some exceptions, and a few tropical ecologists have published more accessible and personal accounts of their fieldwork. I recommend the following:

Goulding, M. *Amazon, The Flooded Forests*. London: BBC Books, 1989.

Snow, D. *The Web of Adaptation*. New York: Demeter Press-Quadrangle, 1976.

Tropical ecologist John Terborgh's latest book, *Where Have All the Birds Gone?* (Princeton, New Jersey: Princeton University Press, 1989), is another exception to my above generalization.

A uniquely elegant and profound book that discusses tropical fieldwork, the importance of biological diversity, the nature of science and our relationship to nature is sociobiologist E.O. Wilson's *Biophilia* (Cambridge, Massachusetts: Harvard University Press, 1984).

Those concerned with tropical conservation will find a good introduction in the following books:

Bunker, S.G. *Underdeveloping the Amazon*. Chicago: University of Chicago Press, 1985.

Caufield, C. *In the Rainforest*. London: Heinmann, 1985.

Myers, N. *The Primary Source: Tropical Forest and Our Future*. New York: Norton, 1984.

Soule, M. *Conservation Biology: The Science of Scarcity and Diversity*. Sunderland, Massachusetts: Sinauer, 1986.

Wilson, E. (ed.). *Biodiversity*. Washington, D.C.: National Academy Press, 1988.

For those who wish to delve into tropical ecological research, the following books will get you started, and they contain references to most of the previous important technical literature:

Janzen, D. (ed.). *Costa Rican Natural History*. Chicago: University of Chicago Press, 1983.

Prance, G.T., and T. Lovejoy (eds.). *Amazonia*. New York: Pergamon Press, 1985.

INDEX

Agriculture and soil depletion, 72-73
Antbirds, 102-103
Anteaters
    compared with sloths, 124
    tamandua, 94-95
Anthropomorphism, 24-25
Ants, army, as beaters for cryptic prey, 102-103
Atta leaf-cutting ants, 69-70
Avocado, wild, seed dispersal, 57, 58
Beaters for cryptic prey, 101-103
Beetles
    meloid, chemical defence, 129
    rove, chemical defence, 127-128
Bellbird, courtship and breeding behaviour, 58-59
Birds
    food resources, 16-17
    species diversity, 16-17
Bocachica, fishing for, 148
Bromeliads and species diversity, 22
Bushmaster, camouflage, 108
Butterflies
    ithomiine, chemical defence, 135
    puddling, 70
    soil eating, 70
Caffeine, 88
Caiman, 116-117
Calathea insignis, 77-78

Calcium deficiency in tropical soils, 71-72
Calls of frogs, 31-32
Camouflage, 98-109
Cantharidin, 129
Caterpillars, chemical defence, 130
Catfish, 115
Chemical defence mechanisms, 52-53, 54-55, 84-85,
   87, 126-135
Climate
   and frogs, 25-27
   and species diversity, 19-20
Coevolution, 74-83
Coloration, adaptive, 98-109
Colour
   in camouflage, 105
   in chemical defence, 130
Courtship and breeding behaviour as affected by
   fruit, 58-59
Cryptic camouflage, 98, 99-101, 103-108
Cucumber beetles, chemical defence, 134
Curare, 87-88
Cyanide, 130-131
Dart poisons, 85, 87
Defecation
   howler monkeys', 124-125
   sloths', 124-125
Defence mechanisms

   chemical, 52-53, 54-55, 84-85, 87, 126-135
   termites', 96
Deforestation and fish populations, 117
Discovery of rainforest resources, 84-91
Dispersal of fruit seeds, 53-58
Diversity of species
   and rarity, 35
   in tropical habitats, 14-23
Durian, 52-53
Ecological interdependence, 74-83
Ecology, difficulty of understanding, 149
Edibility of tropical fruits, 53-54
Epiphytes and species diversity, 18-19, 20-22
Extinction and geographical rarity, 39-41
Feeding behaviour
   of fer-de-lance, 48-49
   of frogs, 31
   of keel-billed toucans, 56-57
   of oilbirds, 57
   and prehensile tails, 62-66
   of quetzals, 57-58
   of snakes, 43-49
   of spider monkeys, 58
Fer-de-lance
   camouflage, 108
   feeding behaviour, 48-49
Fish

in Amazonia, 110-117
and forest flooding, 112-114, 117
Food resources and species diversity of birds, 16-17
Forest destruction and fish populations, 117
Forest flooding and fish, 112-114, 117
Forest structure and species diversity, 17-18
Frogs, 24-33
    for dart poison, 85, 87
    poisonous skin secretions, 84-85
Fruits, 52-59
    chemical defences, 52-53, 54-55
Geographical specialization and rarity, 37-41
Geophagy, 69-71
Global warming and termites, 96-97
Habitat loss and jaguars, 141
Hallucinogens, 89-90
Heliconia
    ecological role of, 75-83
    and hermit hummingbird, 75-80
    miniature ponds in, 82
    shelter in, 82-83
Hoatzin, compared with sloths, 124
Humans, geophagy in, 70
Humidity
    and frogs, 25-27
    and species diversity, 19-20
Hummingbird, hermit, 74

and heliconias, 75-80
    foraging strategy, 80
Hummingbird flower mites, 80
Indian cultures of Peru, 146-147
Indigenous knowledge of rainforest resources, 84-91
Jaguar, 136-141
Kinkajou, prehensile tail of, 63
Large-seed dispersal, 56-58
Leaf-eaters' role in rainforest food chain, 125
Lianas and species diversity, 20-21
Low-density rarity, 36
Macaws, geophagy in, 70-71
Magical properties of living species, 90-91
Manú National Park, 142-149
Migratory fish, 113-114
Millipedes, chemical defence, 130-131
Mineral deficiencies in tropical forests, 68-73
Monkeys
    howler, compared with sloths, 124-125
    prehensile tails of, 62-63
    spider, feeding behaviour, 58
Mouths, snakes', 44-47
Nest building and prehensile tails, 66
Oilbird, feeding behaviour, 57
Olingo, prehensile tail of, 63
Opossum, prehensile tail of, 63
Pacu, 110-112

Palenque, Rio, 40-41
Panthera onca, 136-141
Parasites and species diversity, 22-23
Parrots, geophagy in, 70-71
Pederin, 127-128
Phyllobates frogs, poisonous skin secretions, 84-85
Piranha, 115-116
Plants
  chemical defences, 52-53, 54-55, 87, 131, 133-135
  used for dart poison, 87-88
Poisons
  from frogs, 85
  from plants, 87-88, 131, 133-135
Porcupine, prehensile tail of, 60-61
Predators
  use of camouflage, 108
  of frogs, 27
  keystone, 141
  techniques for finding cryptic prey, 100-103
Prehensile tails, 60-67
Prey size, snakes', 44
Quetzal, feeding behaviour, 57-58
Rainforest resources, discovery of, 84-91
Raoism, 88-89
Rarity, 34-41
Reproductive activities of frogs, 27-31
Search images, 103

Seed-dispersal strategies of fruit trees, 54-58
Sloths, 118-125
Small-seed dispersal, 55-56
Snakes, 42-51
  prehensile tails of, 66
Songs of frogs, 31-32
Specialization
  and rarity, 36-37
  and species diversity, 17
Species diversity
  and rarity, 35
  in tropical habitats, 14-23
Spider monkey, feeding behaviour, 58
Startle reflex, 43
Stink bugs, chemical defence, 130
Tails, prehensile, 60-67
Tamanduas, 94-95
Termites, 92-97
  defence, 96
  and global warming, 96-97
Toucan, keel-billed, feeding behaviour, 56-57
Treehopper, 80
Urbanization and soil depletion in the Tropics,
  72-73
Venom, snake, 47-50
  resistance to, 49-50
Wasps, chemical defence, 133

CREDITS

All photographs other than those listed below were taken by Michael and Patricia Fogden.

P.86 Stephanie Dinkins/Photo Researchers, Inc.; p.87 G. Harrison/Bruce Coleman, Inc.; p.88 G. Harrison/Bruce Coleman, Inc.; p.90 Mark J. Plotkin; p.91 Hanbury-Tenison/Robert Harding Picture Library; p.110 Tom McHugh, Steinhart Aquarium/Photo Researchers, Inc.; p.110 André Bärtschi; p.112 Mark J. Plotkin; p.113 Michael Goulding, Partridge Films Ltd./Oxford Scientific Films; p.114 Loren McIntyre; p.115 Warwick Johnson/Oxford Scientific Films; p.117 Loren McIntyre.